Mary Timothy Prokes

MUTUALITY

The Human Image of Trinitarian Love

PAULIST PRESS
New York/Mahwah, N.J.

ACKNOWLEDGMENTS

The excerpt from Christopher Fry's "The Lady's Not For Burning" from *Christopher Fry Plays,* London: Oxford University Press, copyright © 1973 is reprinted by permission of Oxford University Press, Inc., New York.

Excerpts from *I and Thou* by Martin Buber, translated by Walter Kaufmann are reprinted for publication with the permission of Charles Scribner's Sons, an imprint of Macmillan Publishing Company. Translation copyright © 1970 Charles Scribner's Sons. Publication of these excerpts for the rest of the World has been granted by T. and T. Clark, Ltd. Publishers, Edinburgh.

Library of Congress Cataloging-in-Publication Data

Prokes, Mary Timothy, 1931–
Mutuality: the human image of trinitarian love/Mary Timothy Prokes.
p. cm.
Includes bibliographical references and index.
ISBN 0-8091-3443-8 (pbk.)
1. Trinity. 2. Spiritual life–Catholic authors. 3. Interpersonal relations–Religious aspects–Catholic Church. 4. Church renewal–Catholic Church. 5. Catholic Church–Doctrines. I. Title.
BT111.2.P765 1993
231'.044–dc20 93-36047
CIP

Published by Paulist Press
997 Macarthur Boulevard
Mahwah, New Jersey 07430

Printed and bound in the
United States of America

Contents

Dedicated
in grateful praise
to
the Perichoretic Three-in-One

Preface

Pure
love frees the heart
like rain swinging from willow
wands

–Sister Maura Eichner, SSND[1]

The exultant cry, "O Marvelous Exchange! Man's Creator has become man, born of a Virgin!" recurs in the prayer of the church for the feast of Mary, Mother of God. It celebrates the incarnation in terms of a self-giving encounter between the divine and the human. In his incarnate presence on earth, Jesus Christ revealed that the inner life of the One God is *itself* a "Marvelous Exchange" of divine personal self-gift. His saving gift of self brought the possibility of purified love, freeing the human heart into a giving and receiving that images divine life.

This is a book about mutuality, that reciprocal self-gift that is foundational for a spirituality of interpersonal relationships. It is also an attempt to bring a "marvelous exchange" between this "*theology of gift*" and daily Christian life. The specific terms and categories of trinitarian theology are brought into relation with specific persons, places and events that are tangible at the conclusion of the twentieth century. Too often serious theological reflection on the intimate life of the Trinity remains abstract, removed from the particulars of Christian spiritual life.

While inclusive language has been employed whenever possible, there has been no alteration of cited texts in this regard, and the scripturally-received names of Father, Son and Holy Spirit have been retained throughout.

It is my hope that this reflection on mutuality brings fresh theological insight regarding: 1) the specific manner in which the church images trinitarian exchange; 2) the meaning of *gift* as the ultimate category of being; 3) the relation between mutuality and incongruity; and 4) vital examples of lived mutuality.

I thank all who entered into "marvelous exchanges" during the research and writing of this book. In particular I thank those who granted interviews: Joseph Cardinal Ratzinger; Paola Piscitelli and the Community of St. Egidio; DeVon Cunningham and members of St. Cecilia Parish; Fr. Douglas Mosey, CSB; the Sponsor Couples Community; the Franciscan Sisters of the Eucharist; the Abbess and Community of the Abbey of Regina Laudis; and the Caretaker on Robert Leather Road. Gratitude is extended to all who facilitated research, especially my community, the School Sisters of Notre Dame; St. Thomas More College (that granted a sabbatical leave); Sister Sarah Doser, FSE; Drs. Victoria Krizsan and Donald McIver; the library staffs at St. Thomas More College, Saskatoon; St. Paul's University, Ottawa; and the Library of Congress, Washington, D.C. Particular thanks to Margaret and Dr. Robert Sanche who enabled preparation of the manuscript for publication; to Dr. Stephen and Joanne Sanche and Judy Classen for their technical assistance; and to my family for their continual support.

CHAPTER ONE

Mutuality and the Fullness of Time

> Certainly in mutual and very fervent love nothing is rarer or more magnificent than to wish that another be loved equally by the one whom you love supremely and by whom you are supremely loved.
>
> –*Richard of St. Victor* [1]

Yearly, on the Feast of the Holy Trinity, many homilists express difficulty in relating this central mystery to the experience of those who celebrate it. Some allude to it almost apologetically, as if the doctrine is too abstract to have any relevance in daily life. This dilemma among homilists is symptomatic of a widespread lack of understanding regarding trinitarian life. That is not surprising. In promising the gift of the Holy Spirit, Jesus said that he still had many things to tell his followers, "but they would be too much for you now."[2] Although he had spoken passionately of the relationships he shared with the Father and the Spirit, Jesus indicated that the unfolding and understanding of his message would require assistance and time. The abiding Holy Spirit would be the one to lead them "to the complete truth" and tell of "the things to come" after his death and resurrection (cf. Jn 16:13).

Any advance into "the complete truth" awaits a certain fullness of time, unpredictable by human calculations. When this happens under the guidance of the Holy Spirit, that which has been familiar, even routine, becomes fresh and vibrant. The Second Vatican Council marked such a "fullness of time." Within the all-encompassing renewal evoked by the council, there was a specific, new expression of the universal call to holiness. It was simultaneously the call for a depth spirituality suitable for nourishing such holiness in the contemporary world.

In a landmark article written shortly after the council, Ewert Cousins identified a definite turning point in this regard. He wrote: "The shift from a spirituality of 'isolationism' or 'rugged individualism' to a community-based spirituality has occurred so fast that theologians have been taken off guard."[3] There was a new theological task: that of providing doctrinal and theological underpinnings for a *spirituality of interpersonal relations.* Cousins suggested that theologians might begin by consulting the work of a twelfth-century theologian, Richard of St. Victor. Cousins found that the Victorine's insights regarding the inner life of the Trinity had "considerable resonance with trends on the contemporary scene." In fact, he conjectured that Richard's *De Trinitate* had penetrated into areas not fully drawn into his consciousness, but which were extremely relevant now in the later twentieth century:

> Although he [Richard of St. Victor] has provided much material for a theology of interpersonal relations, his thought remains seminal and open. It can suggest to contemporary theologians ways of integrating into their vision the findings of psychoanalysis, phenomenology and existentialism. Or it can point to directions that Richard had only partly explored, or it can suggest entirely new areas for theologians to investigate in developing a contemporary theology of interpersonal relations.[4]

Ewert Cousins was aware that a breakthrough had occurred, enabling Christians to perceive that trinitarian life was the basis for a spirituality of interpersonal relations. A generation has passed since he identified the shift to a community-based spirituality and many books have already been devoted to the theme. While *mutuality* has been introduced in some of these works, it is still an area "only partly explored," needing explication, since mutual relations among divine persons are the basis for a contemporary spirituality rooted in interpersonal relations.

This book is intended, then, as an introduction to *mutuality* both within the Trinity and among the people of God. To do this, it is necessary 1) to reflect in an introductory manner on the Christian understanding of mutual self-gift among the persons of the Trinity, and then 2) to explore the possibility of reciprocal self-gift being embodied in daily life. The book is both speculative and pastoral—an attempt to enflesh theology. Since all reflection emerges from a given perspective, it is helpful from the outset to set a context.

Setting the Context

This work on mutuality emerges from the Roman Catholic tradition, which I consider a gift rather than a restraint. Being "on-line" with the tradition is analogous to an astronaut's unbroken communication with ground control personnel, allowing a spacewalker to venture into the unknown. Analogously, being "on-line" with the magisterium allows a theologian to press into horizons of mystery and interdisciplinary speculation without spinning into orbits of personal idiosyncrasy.

The prime reference for understanding mutuality is the giving and receiving of person-gift within the Blessed Trinity. As will be shown, this exchange is more than the basis of an interpersonal spirituality; it is the basis of *all* reality. I have called reflection on this mutual giving and receiving of person-gift, together with its image in human relations, a "*Donum theology*," or a theology of gift. Donald Gelpi points to the bond between divine mutual relations and human experience, saying of divine Persons:

> [Their] identity of life is achieved by Their perfect mutual inexistence. And Their mutual inexistence results from Their perfect mutual self-donation to one another in the supreme perfection of selfless love. Finally, we have discovered in the analogy of experience a way of making both the mutual inexistence of the divine persons and Their identity of life thinkable.[5]

Since the present work is concerned with mutuality, I will not dwell on general theological theories and doctrinal development regarding the Trinity. The approach here is speculative, an attempt to press into the horizon of mystery, which, like the living cell, is "semi-permeable": What is consonant with the living mystery of God is offered as a contribution; what is nonadmissable is open to correction and change. Often, theological inquiry is illumined by insights from other disciplines. Like the tapper of maple trees, the speculative theologian must open numerous sources and then relentlessly boil and integrate what has been received in order to achieve a new synthesis. It is important to note that the citing of a helpful source does not imply support of an author's entire system of thought.

A theology of mutuality must relate to human life in practical, tangible ways. Every human person, created in the image of God, is called to share in the exchange of divine person-gift. The very meaning of "spirituality" hinges on this possibility within the human transactions of daily life. Jesus slowly revealed aspects of mutuality in God-life within the larger context of washing feet and putting spittled clay on sightless eyes. A theology of interpersonal relations today must apply to breakfast conversations across cereal boxes and to complex negotiations concerning those who are threatened, maimed and starving and who await even glimmers of mutual love.

In *Trinity and Society*, Leonardo Boff writes:

> There is a renewal of trinitarian thought taking place now...on the links that bind women and men together in community and society–links that also involve the Persons of the Trinity. Society is not just the sum total of the individuals that make it up, but has its own being woven out of the threads of relationships among individuals, functions and institutions, which together make up the social and political community.... So human society is a pointer on the road to the mystery of the Trinity, while the mystery of the Trinity, as we know it from revelation, is a pointer toward social life and its archetype. Human society holds a *vestigium Trinitatis* since the Trinity is "the divine society."[6]

That is why the present work has the twofold purpose introduced above: 1) to open the meaning of mutuality in its prime realization within trinitarian life, and 2) to explore its meaning in a sacramental world, in the midst of human life. For this "theology of gift" to be helpful in providing what Cousins called "theological and doctrinal underpinnings" for a spirituality of interpersonal relations, it must be tangible, able to be recognized within experience. Every human expression of mutuality will be partial and flawed. In relating theology to life, however, it is helpful to reflect on examples (admittedly imperfect) that allow an applied exploration of lived mutuality. That is why a significant part of preparing this work was devoted to field research, the attempt to find expressions of mutuality within small communities, in parish life, and in human relationships with the earth. The final chapters of this book are the result of this research into the application of a *Donum* theology, revealing its meaning in areas as diverse as liturgy, cosmetology and farming.

Mutuality and the Fullness of Time

Before reflecting on mutuality within God-life, we must ask what the term *mutuality* means. Like many basic words, *mutuality* is defined variously. Its roots are found in Middle English, Middle French and Latin. The adjective "mutual" can refer to what is gained or received in equal amount, or it can indicate what two or more persons do, possess or experience. In dictionary terms, the noun "mutuality" is defined as the "quality or state of being mutual: the quality of reciprocity."[7] Words like "interchange," "interaction" and "interdependence" serve as synonyms for "mutuality." As it is theologically explored in the present work, however, *the pristine meaning of mutuality is understood as the perfect reciprocal giving and receiving among trinitarian Persons.* Mutuality signifies a principle of unity in which there is neither domination, nor exclusion, nor loss of personal identity. Every creaturely form of mutuality is an image of this divine paradigm which has implications not only for humans in their interactions with one another, but also for all nonpersonal creatures.

Before considering the meaning of reciprocal self-gift in the Trinity and in human relations, however, it is important to ask why the late twentieth century has proved to be a certain "fullness of time" for understanding mutuality. If every significant advance or initiative waits upon the time of readiness, what in the present moment impels us toward a breakthrough in understanding mutuality? Among the so-called developed nations of the west there is a turbulent confluence occurring between two seemingly incompatible streams of thought and action: 1) there is, on the one hand, a relentless drive toward consummate individual fulfillment and 2) there is a multifaceted search for new forms of union. It is useful to characterize these two pursuits briefly in assessing that a certain fullness of time has come for a deepened realization of mutuality.

The drive for individual fulfillment gained momentum during the so-called "modern age" (an awkward designation for the past four to five centuries). Scientific and technical achievements accompanied a strong emphasis on the individual person, on specific nations and groups. The modern age glorified personal achievement and the overcoming of traditional political, social and religious restraints. Especially after the Enlightenment, it seemed that human reason and perfected techniques would bring inevitable progress. Impressive advances were made. But, as Peter Henrici points out, the actual result has not been unremitting liberation and advance. Too often, human life is *determined* by inventions and technical interventions. Henrici says that within the realm of ideas and awareness, there have been two major developments:

> There is above all the modern consciousness of progress, for, while ideas are supplanted and superseded, technical inventions tend to accumulate. Secondly, the ability to make things becomes the predominant idea. Natural science originated as a subsequent theoretical foundation for an already accomplished technology.... Nature was no longer a marvelous wonder; rather it was material for human creativity.... man no longer enjoys the luxury of being able to surrender "calmly" and contemplatively to the cosmic order; he has to continue making things: technologically, scientifically, politically.... His most significant tool is his reason which is, consequently, transformed into an instrumental reason.[8]

In one sense, the modern age can be characterized as a turn from the "within" to the "without." Perhaps nothing brought this about more surely than communication at the speed of light. Television has dissolved many of the familiar boundaries of space and time. In North American suburbs viewers can eat dinner in the electronic presence of Ethiopians languishing in the African desert. Along with supper, television viewers can absorb the destruction of rain forests, or an astronaut's attempt to grasp an errant satellite. It is the nature of telecommunications to evoke instant awareness, and wherever there is a dramatic awakening of consciousness, interpersonal relationships are affected. Because contact at the speed of light is disembodied from the specifics of time, place and context, television viewers can imperceptibly become indifferent to the personal dimension of world events. Frequent repetition makes what was formerly "unthinkable" not only thinkable, but seemingly familiar and reasonable. Thus, technological individualism can lead to impersonal manipulation at a distance. From the isolated privacy of home or office, unconscionable computer hackers can violate persons and information.[9]

In spite of the immense potential of science and technology, then, we have arrived at a time of disenchantment regarding inevitable fulfillment and progress. The surface of the world community is like a geyser park where disturbances which have been burbling beneath the surface are erupting suddenly in heated release. With so many persons, groups and nations awakened to the possibilities of individual fulfillment, the satisfaction of one becomes a threat to the others. As a result, many individuals and groups are seeking their unique fulfillment through *separation* from the larger community. This withdrawal is accompanied by an emphasis on legal protection of individual rights. From within and outside the church community comes the cry that traditional structures must crumble to make way for a still undetermined "new world order" that will somehow correct the present situation. The euphoria over unlimited individual fulfillment has eroded, but the way to new forms of union is unclear.

It is now commonplace to say that the modern age has given way to the "postmodern age." There is no precise definition of this term. For some it indicates disillusionment with the relentless press toward individualism. For others it means an individualism *so* replete that it separates persons and words at the very level of meaning. An example of the latter can be found in the work of French "deconstructionist," Jacques Derrida. In the words of Kenneth Schmitz, Derrida "harries" significant texts from the western tradition "in order to *decenter, destabilize,* and *defer* their meaning."[10] In "decentering," Derrida does not transfer a text's basic meaning from one center to another: he denies that the text has any center at all and exploits a text's resources against itself. Derrida holds that an author's intention does not unify a work. Words have meaning only when used with other words, so *meaning* is postponed until this placement occurs. In this deconstructionist approach, there is no equivalence between signified and signifier. Words are like jetsam bobbing on a vast sea; now touching here, now touching there, always without consistent referents. Kenneth Schmitz writes:

> Deconstruction renounces the centrality of self. In the view of deconstruction, meaning is not constructed through self-reference; nor is it built up through reference to an other opposed to the self in binary opposition as dialectics and structuralism have it. Meaning has no resting place, no stopping point within or outside the text, no transcendental signified or signifier which can stop the endless chain of supplementary meanings.[11]

There is a correlation between deconstructionist theory and the frequent disengagement of word and meaning in advertising. Dorothee Soelle has observed that religious language which used to express the deepest human needs now sells products. It is a blasphemous use of religious language, she says, free of memories, threats and wounds:

> The slogan for Levi jeans, "Thou shalt have no other jeans before me," captures the spirit of the second industrial revolution and the mutation of values that is accrued from it.... People are cut off from the rhythm of nature. Our need for a renewal of life also disappears, and we forget our need for rest after working, for night after day, for cleansing after pollution, and for stillness after noise.... Religious language transmits a sharing of hope with others, as well as what I call the emphatic understanding of life. The public death of this language and its replacement by the public language of advertising is a major cultural event.[12]

If the longing for individual fulfillment is severed from transcendent meaning, there is fragmentation rather than integral individuation. Linguistic theory is imitating life: the all too common experience of disengagement and isolation. This is not to say that dissonance and destabilization are twentieth century inventions. In fact, new life and possibility require a disturbing of the status quo. What is novel in recent times, however, is the conviction that *destabilization is an end in itself,* a strategy for unmasking the seeming "meaninglessness of it all." Cynicism over the failure of technology to effect fulfillment has led to the search for control over one's person and environment. If words—and life itself—lack inherent meaning, it is still possible to relish *control* as an expression of individual worth. For example, the late British clergyman, Leslie Weatherhead, said: "We do not leave birth to God.... We space births. We prevent births. We arrange births. Man should learn to become the lord of death as well as the master of birth."[13] But fragmentation and the endeavor to control one's existence are not the only forces at work in the postmodern age.

The Search for Union: A Longing for Mutual Relations

The second major current of thought and action today is the search for union. It takes many forms. Despite the widespread denial of meaning and transcendence, many are convinced that union is possible: within the human person, among persons, between the signified and the signifier. One finds this longing expressed in unexpected ways: in conversations among strangers waiting for flight connections; in films that treat of supernatural occurrences; in the New Age predilection for personal guides and for integration with the past. Humanity is like a dog sniffing the air for an unseen Presence. If telecommunications frequently contribute to the fragmentation of human life, they also have the enormous potential to enable unity among peoples. It is becoming obsolete to separate the world community into "east" and "west," or even to speak of first, second and third worlds, when all nations mingle in the satellite dish.

The growing realization of the need for global interdependence and responsibility is often driven by the desire for survival, but there are deeper, lasting insights emerging. Surprisingly, some derive from scientific research. Sophisticated instruments indicate that there is a field quality about the universe that defies separation into discrete, isolated areas. Within the material, unconscious level of creation there is a teeming interflow of the seen and unseen, of being and becoming in which even the smallest physical events have a lasting impact upon one another. In his book *Chaos*, James Gleick explains a term coined by global weather forecasters: the Butterfly Effect. It is "the notion that a butterfly stirring the air today in Peking can transform storm systems next month in New York."[14] International forecasters found that weather predictions made two or three days in advance were merely speculative; those made six or seven days ahead were worthless. Small disturbances multiply, says Gleick, and "In science as in life, it is well known that a chain of events can have a point of crisis that could magnify small changes."[15] We are gradually coming to appreciate the interrelatedness of all things. Both micro and macro events within creation prompt reflection on the universal call to union.

Astronaut James Irwin, in retrospect of his journey to the moon, said that from his spacecraft the earth resembled a Christmas tree ornament hung against the darkness. "As we flew into space we had a new sense of ourselves, of the earth, and of the nearness of God."[16] Having achieved individual technical excellence in his personal life, Irwin was open to new levels of union:

> We were outside of ordinary reality; I sensed the beginning of some sort of deep change taking place inside of me. Looking back at that spaceship we call earth, I was touched by a desire to convince man that he has a unique place to live, that he is a unique creature, and that he must learn to live with his neighbors.[17]

From Irwin's account, it is evident that self-fulfillment and the search for union are not inherently incompatible. In fact, genuine interpersonal relationship requires a reasonable level of self-fulfillment as the basis for reciprocal giving and receiving. Despite the multiple forms of twisted and broken relationships, despite wars and violence, there endures a conviction that genuine interpersonal union is possible. For persons of faith, the turbulent confluence between individual fulfillment and the desire for union signals a breakthrough point for receptivity to trinitarian mutuality and its human counterpart. For many Christians, the God in whose image they profess to be created remains a remote mystery having scant relevance for daily life. Yet it is that mystery that has *everything* to do with understanding *both* individual fulfillment and personal communion. Jesus Christ revealed that the One God is neither an isolated monad nor a self-absorbed dyad, but a personal communion: Father, Son and Holy Spirit. To be created in the image of God, then, is to be created for interpersonal communion. This must be pondered anew in every age, but especially at breakthrough moments of awareness. It is not surprising, then, that in recent decades there has been heightened theological interest in the mutual indwelling of the divine persons. Traditionally, this loving interchange has been termed *perichoresis* (a Greek word meaning "mutual interpenetration") or *circuminsession* (a Latin word meaning literally "sitting in each other"). What these terms represent is crucial for a faith understanding of mutuality in its divine and human expressions.

It is also not surprising that in the late 1970s Pope John Paul II began to devote his weekly audiences to the basic meaning of interpersonal relations. He plumbed the human vocation for union, beginning with the Genesis accounts of woman and man created in the image and likeness of God.[18] Walter Ong maintains that the entire history of human consciousness can be plotted by the ongoing female-male dialectic that comes to a new synthesis in each age.[19] It may be that the theological question underlying our own age's synthesis is this: *How is inner trinitarian life paradigmatic for relationships between women and men–and for all interpersonal communion?*

The growing answers to this question cannot remain abstract. It is necessary to suggest examples and analogies that reveal from various perspectives *something* of the correspondence between divine and human relationships. Intimations of God's inner life have been revealed in the flesh. Through Jesus' shared prayer and intimate sharing, the first disciples learned of his relationship with the Father and the Spirit. Revelation occurred in the ordinary context of eating, fishing and traveling. We can do no better as we grapple with concepts, words and our own poverty of relationships. It is essential that theology be in active interchange with life, and the more profound the mystery, the greater the need for numerous images and examples to illumine it. There is always the danger of fastening upon one favorite example to the exclusion of others (as the Kenyan proverb has it: I pointed out the moon to you, but all you saw was my finger).

The task in the present work, then, involves two things: 1) exploring the meaning of mutuality in trinitarian relations in order to perceive anew the human vocation to live as image of this divine mutual love; and 2) providing examples of mutuality within the church that (imperfect as they are) put flesh on this image in our own time, in particular places, among very specific people. Among the many examples that might serve in this regard, I have selected the following from my fieldwork: the St. Egidio Community of Rome, for its amazing origins among young women and men and their mutuality with the poor; the Sponsor Couples, a small community of married couples in the eastern United States, for the mutual mission they share; St. Cecilia Parish in the inner city of Detroit, for its experiment in living the mutuality of ordained and lay priesthood; and Regina Laudis Abbey, Bethlehem, Connecticut, for its lived mutuality with "the land." I have termed this union of reflection upon perichoretic love and its application in life a "*Donum* theology" or a "theology of gift," since both divine and human expressions of mutuality stem from person-gift. As will be seen later, the giving and receiving of person-gift is so foundational that *gift* can be designated the most basic category of existence. First, however, what is meant by saying that all mutuality takes its origin in trinitarian relations?

CHAPTER TWO

Intimate Trinitarian Life: Total Gift

> It can be said that in the Holy Spirit the intimate life of the Triune God becomes totally gift, an exchange of mutual love between the divine Persons, and that through the Holy Spirit God exists in the mode of gift.... The Holy Spirit, being consubstantial with the Father and the Son in divinity, is love and uncreated gift from which derives as from its source (*fons vivus*) *all giving of gifts* vis-à-vis creatures (created gift): the gift of existence to all things through creation; the gift of grace to human beings through the whole economy of salvation.
>
> –*On the Holy Spirit in the Life of the Church and the World* [1]

Among the multitude of sources that describe trinitarian life, several are particularly helpful for an understanding of mutuality: the last discourse in the gospel of John; selected writings of St. Augustine and Richard of St. Victor; and portions of twentieth century works that bring fresh imagery and understanding to the trinitarian mystery. In them one finds that divine mutuality is identified with person-gift; that it requires a divine "third"; and that it is open to human participation. It is from this divine mutuality that all human forms of mutual self-gift take their meaning.

While the Hebrew Testament does not refer explicitly to personal relations within the One God,[2] the New Testament describes Jesus as revealing the inner relations of God progressively through his prayer, teaching and life. He was revelation in the flesh. So he spoke familiarly of the Father and the Spirit within the context of meals and journeys, using images and words that were comprehensible, at least in kernel, to his contemporaries. In the unfolding of ordinary life, he prepared his disciples to receive ever-deepening insights into divine relationships. The culmination of this revelation, however, came in his farewell discourse (John, Ch. 13–17) at the last supper. In this intense pre-death revelation, Jesus spoke intimately of the personal communion among the Father, the Son and the Holy Spirit. For centuries, the church would grapple with this revelation regarding divine personal love, equality, and identity, each early ecumenical council trying to formulate in the technical language of theology what had been conveyed so personally at the supper. The glimpse into divine life, shared in Christ's farewell discourse, is still redolent of a spring paschal evening and the bittersweet imparting of last words to friends.

In his commentary on the fourth gospel, Royce Gordon Gruenler notes how Jesus protected the integrity of each divine Person and avoided any suggestion of tritheism.[3] In his public life Jesus had spoken repeatedly of his unique relationship with the Father, but in his farewell, he shared how intimately he and the Father were in union with the "Advocate," the "Spirit of Truth" whom they would send. The Holy Spirit would not speak "as from himself" but would take what is of Jesus, what he had received from the Father, and help the disciples to understand it. Jesus spoke of the Paraclete as "another counselor," Jesus himself being their first counselor. In brief, cogent revelation the disciples heard that the first and second counselors are at-one in giving and receiving, listening and speaking. In his encyclical on the Holy Spirit, Pope John Paul II writes, "Thus in the farewell discourse at the Last Supper, we can say that *the highest point of the revelation of the Trinity* is reached."[4]

Royce Gruenler ruminates on the interchangeability of authority, truthspeaking and glorification among the divine Persons, as described in John 16:14–15.[5] Jesus spoke of inner God-life in terms of equality and mutual deference. There is no competition among divine Persons:

> The Spirit defers in serving the Son as he serves the community of believers. The Father is for the moment in the background. Jesus then explicitly claims correlativity with the Father, repeating the theme that the Holy Spirit takes what is the Son's and declares it to the disciples. It is the

nature of the Triune Community that Father, Son and Holy Spirit share equally together.[6]

To assist his disciples in grasping their own potential for sharing in this mystery of enduring union, Jesus used the familiar images of grapevine and home. They were to remain in union with him as branches on a living vine. But in startlingly intimate terms, he urged: "Make your home in me, as I make mine in you" (Jn 15:4). Jesus transcended the usual patterns of home and dwelling place. No longer were his followers to identify the temple as the "divine residence." For his followers, to be "at home" meant a mutual indwelling among divine and human persons.

Mutual Indwelling

The word *menein*, used in the last discourse, means to remain, abide, dwell on, or stay, in the sense of being intimately united to someone. Raymond Brown points out that Jesus opened the possibility of this indwelling not only to those immediately at table with him, but also to those who would later respond to this invitation:

> To remain in Jesus, or in the Father, or in one of the divine attributes or gifts is intimately associated with keeping the commandments in a spirit of love (John xv 10; I John iv 12, 16), with a struggle against the world (I John ii 16–17), and with bearing fruit (John xv 5)–all basic Christian duties. Thus indwelling is not the exclusive experience of chosen souls within the Christian community; it is the essential constitutive principle of all Christian life.[7]

The potential for union revealed by Jesus is not limited to the Twelve and a few privileged mystics. Neither, however, is it an automatic possession of Jesus' followers, or a sentimental bond. The Johannine text indicates that indwelling is linked with keeping Jesus' words, with "recognizing" the gift being offered. Raymond Brown says that the Greek word *theorein,* used by John for "seeing," applies to both bodily and spiritual sight and "the failure to accept and the failure to see or recognize constitute an attitude."[8] That is why the "world" cannot recognize the Spirit, while Jesus' own are capable of that recognition "because he is with you, he is in you" (Jn 14:17). They are also able to receive Jesus' saying: "I am in my Father and you in me and I in you" (Jn 14:20). There is a threefold indwelling assured in the fourteenth chapter of John's gospel:

> In 15–17 it is the Paraclete/Spirit who will come to dwell within the disciples. In 18–21 it is Jesus who will come to dwell within the disciples. In 23–24.... it is the Father who will come along with Jesus to make a dwelling place within the disciples. Thus seemingly there is a triadic pattern here placing in rough parallelism the Spirit, Jesus, and the Father (with Jesus).[9]

It is increasingly common to find the Trinity described as the "divine community" or the "triune community." Royce Gruenler finds that the attitude among Father, Son and Holy Spirit can be termed a "mutual disposability" or loving deference to one another in perfect equality. Each willingly seeks to serve and please the other. Rather than diminishing their distinctive roles, this mutual deference emphasizes their coinherence as interacting persons. This is the reality intended by the traditional terms *perichoresis* and *circuminsessio,*[10] used to describe the inner life of God which Jesus conveyed in his farewell.

Even more astounding, however, than Jesus' revelation of trinitarian relations was his saying that the divine persons were "at the disposal" of the fledgling community of believers, with Jesus himself as the bonding point for the realization of indwelling, mutual love. Raymond Brown translates John 17:22–23 in the following manner: "that they may be one, just as we are one, I in them and you in me, that they may be brought to completion as one." This is sometimes read anachronistically in reference to the ecumenical movement. Jesus' union with the Father is not a mere moral union, nor is it the result of human activity. Nevertheless, right from the beginning of trinitarian revelation Jesus emphasized the challenging human vocation to share divine interpersonal communion, to be a human community in the image of the three-in-one.

Those gathered in the upper room had the mission of sharing this revelation with people of diverse languages and cultures. It was the beginning of a theological process that will continue to the eschaton, every people receiving the Christian message in their own idiom and contributing to its explication. Unfortunately, the need for precision in formulating the basic tenets of faith *can* result in abstraction, and the intimate sharing of the last supper can be confounded by theological language that has little correlation with life. The mystery of trinitarian union has suffered from such abstraction. Theological reflection utilizes philosophical terms and concepts that are available at a given historical moment and which prove useful in conveying the tenets of faith. Arthur Gibson has shown that Greek philosophy, in some ways so helpful for structuring western Christian thought, also served to dull a Christian sensitivity to trinitarian relations.

Why the Trinity Can Seem Remote

To demonstrate this, Gibson showed how the development of Christian thought in the west took place under the strong influence of Greek philosophy (in its rich variations). Basically, he said, we tend to "think Greek," and that means coming at reality as "essentialists."[11] The basic question for an essentialist is: "What?" In other words, what is this? What can it do? Essentialists place an emphasis on demarcation, on seeing how persons and things *differ* from one another. Such an approach has proved very useful in the development of scientific methods, enabling researchers to analyze and categorize with precision. It is not person-oriented, however. Gibson visualized a "what" as a closed box with clearly defined edges. It is difficult to think of two enclosed "whats" or boxes relating to one another; to imagine *three* "whats" in relationship presents even greater difficulties. The "third" tends to become a satellite of the other two. From this perspective, even the *concept* of Trinity proves troublesome.

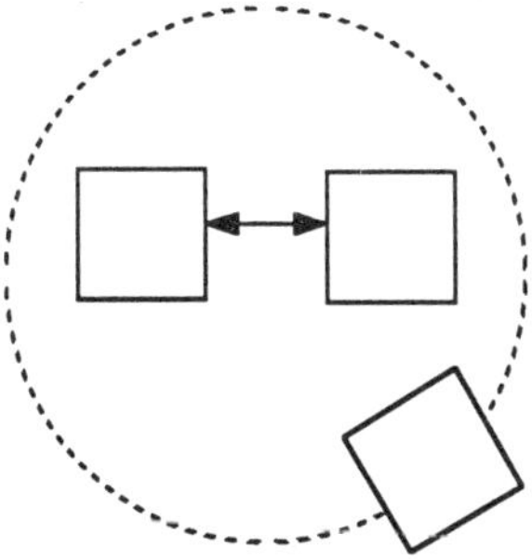

Figure 1.

At the beginning of the twentieth century a philosophical shift occurred and emphasis moved from essence to *existence.* In its manifold forms, "existentialism" brought increased interest in actual existence and interaction. In existentialist terms, the basic question shifted from "what?" to "how?" Arthur Gibson noted that a "what" maintains its individuality in regard to the universe while a "how" is relational. He visualized the existence-oriented "how" as an open circle. In this approach no person or thing is self-contained or isolated. When two or more "hows" relate there is the possibility of dynamic interchange.

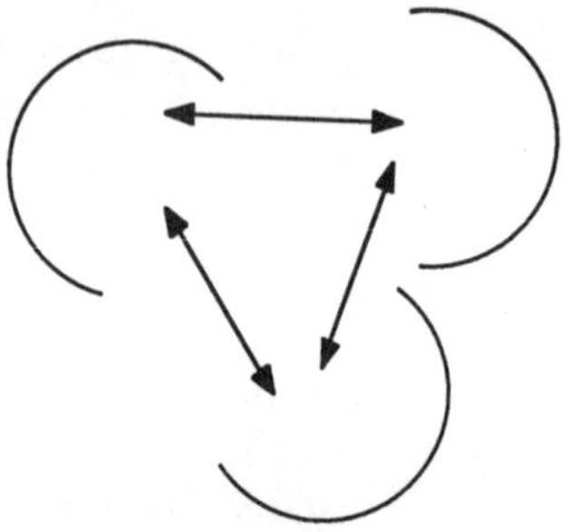

Figure 2.

This is obviously a radical oversimplification of complex philosophical movements, but Gibson, like a deft cartoonist, characterizes one major factor in the west's struggle to relate trinitarian revelation to the human search for both individual fulfillment and interpersonal communion. From an "essentialist" position, it is difficult to see how Father and Son, as two self-enclosed persons, could be in the relationship described by Jesus, and the Holy Spirit as a "third" can seem superfluous. On the other hand, from an "existentialist" perspective, the Father is perceived as moving out in self-gift toward the Son who, in turn, moves out in self-gift to the Father. Both are brought into communion by the vibrant, open personal "third," the Holy Spirit. The Trinity is then understood as dynamic and interrelational.

Movement-toward-the-other is characteristic of divine personality, and it is the ultimate pattern for all relationships. The difficulty of grasping this is sometimes evidenced in subtle ways. For example, the familiar prayer of Augustine, "*Creasti nos ad Te*" is often mistranslated. The small Latin word *ad* means toward, but is usually rendered *for* ("You have created us *for* yourself"). Augustine actually asserted, "You have created us toward yourself."[12] Recently Pope John Paul II said of Augustine: "He sees the human person as a tension directed toward God."[13]

By the time Augustine wrote his *De Trinitate*[14] in the early fifth century, the immanent life of God was described by theologians in terms of 1) *processions* (meaning the Son's eternal birth from the Father and the Holy Spirit's proceeding from Father and Son); 2) *missions* (meaning the manifestations of these eternal processions in creation); 3) *names* (designating the three-in-one); and 4) *relationships* (paternity, filiation and passive spiration). Augustine dealt with these profoundly in his reflections on the Trinity, although he acknowledged that no bodily creature could adequately express how the divine Three worked inseparably.

According to Augustine, that which distinguishes the persons in God is precisely their *relations*. Edmund J. Fortman cautions that Augustine did not identify the persons *as* relations, but showed that the unchangeable relations of paternity, filiation and "gift" are what distinguish them from one another. The scriptures do not speak of divine persons in accidental, changeable ways, but in terms of "unchangeable originational relations."[15] When this is grasped even in elementary ways, the Christian significance of interpersonal relations for human individuation and communion is evident. The distinguishing of persons, divine and human, is rooted in relationships.

To bring the trinitarian mystery closer to life, Augustine sought examples of "trinities" within human experience. He pointed out the psychological triad of mind, self-knowledge and self-love; and the "trinity" in the mind formed by memory, understanding and will. In citing "God is love" (1 Jn 1:5) he said, "Now love is of someone who loves and something is loved with love. So then there are three: the lover, the beloved, and the love" (Bk. 8, Ch. 10). This divine identity as love applies in a particular manner to the Holy Spirit. Augustine says:

> If, then, any one of these three is to be specially called love, what more fitting than that this should be the Holy Spirit?

> In the sense, that is, that in that simple and highest nature, substance is not one thing, and love another thing, but that substance itself is love, and that love itself is substance, whether in the Father, or the Son, or the Holy Spirit, and yet that the Holy Spirit is specially called love. (Bk. 15, Ch. 17).

Since scripture emphasizes that the love of God is poured forth in human hearts through the Holy Spirit, the divine person most appropriately called the love of God is also called the "gift of God." In being-toward one another, divine persons can also be termed "person-gifts." Augustine took care to say, "There is here no subordination of the Gift and no domination of the Givers, but the concord between the Gift and the Givers" (Bk. 15, Ch. 19.36). *Mutuality within the Trinity is a being-toward one another in personal self-gift.*

Richard of St. Victor Describes the Trinity as Perfect Love

In the twelfth century, Richard of St. Victor brought a unique perspective to trinitarian theology. He wrote with the intensity and warmth of an Augustine, but he set out to demonstrate that perfect love *required* a divine Trinity. In Book Three of his *De Trinitate,* where he explored divine identity as *love,* he acknowledged his own vulnerability. Let anyone who wishes laugh or mock, he said, "for if I speak truth here, it is not so much knowledge that lifts me up, but rather the ardor of a burning soul that urges me to try this.... And if it should happen that I fail.... I will have accomplished something at least, if I may truly say: I have done what I could do; 'I have sought and not found him, I have called and he did not answer me' (Song of Songs 5:6)" (Bk. III, Ch. 1).

Richard argued that nothing is more perfect than charity, but self-love cannot be its basis. Perfect charity means other-directedness, and requires a plurality of persons. It would not do for God to have this supreme charity toward a *created* person; that would be a disorder since no creature is to be loved supremely. Perfect mutual love requires equal, divine persons. Writing of mutual relations in God, Richard said:

> However, it is a characteristic of love, and one without which it cannot possibly exist, to wish to be loved much by

> the one whom you love much. Therefore, love cannot be pleasing if it is not also mutual.... However, in mutual love it is absolutely necessary that there be both one who gives love and one who returns love. Therefore one will be the offerer of love and the other the returner of love (Bk. III, Ch. 3).

A "god" who had the fullest benevolence but did not share it would be absurd. The fullness of glory must be shared, said Richard, since nothing is more glorious and magnificent "than to wish to have nothing that you do not wish to share" (Bk. III, Ch. 6). Richard constructed his argument with the care of a stone mason, one element reinforcing the next within the foundation of trinitarian doctrine. Like Augustine, he appealed to the human experience of love, but instead of focusing on the human image, he made the Trinity itself the prime reference for understanding love.

Consistently, Richard underscored the need for *mutuality* in perfect love. In doing so, he stressed the need for equality: each divine person is loved equally and each is equally perfect. Each has the fullness of wisdom, goodness, and every divine perfection. It is extremely difficult for late twentieth-century Christians to receive the meaning of divine equality. Western culture prompts a constant comparison/evaluation of persons and things. One is ranked "better than" the others. The criteria for ranking are often based in economics, efficiency and visual appearance. What is *different* from another can not be perceived as its equal. This difficulty in perceiving an equality-within-difference is crucial in the search for human images of divine mutuality. There must be at least a growing receptivity to the conviction that equality is possible among those who differ in personal gifts and missions.

Perfect Love Requires a "Third"

It was in chapter eleven of his work on the Trinity that Richard of St. Victor took a genuine leap in understanding divine life and love. Perfect divine love, he said, cannot be realized between two divine persons: it requires a "third." Supreme charity means that nothing better can exist and nothing can be lacking to it. It seems, he says, that in perfect charity, one desires that an "other" be loved as oneself. This is clarified in a crucial passage concerning divine mutual love:

> Certainly in mutual and very fervent love nothing is rarer or more magnificent than to wish that another be loved equally by the one whom you love supremely and by whom you are supremely loved.... Therefore it is necessary that each of those loved supremely and loving supremely should search with equal desire for someone who would be mutually loved and with equal concord willingly possess him. Thus you see how the perfection of charity requires a Trinity of persons (Bk. III, Ch. 11).

This is a radical insight, certainly rooted in the last discourse, but brought to new articulation. Perfect love requires a "third." The implications for this among the People of God remain largely untapped to the present. That is why it is essential to find concrete examples in the contemporary church that allow glimpses into the human imaging of trinitarian mutuality, as wounded and partial as those examples may be. After Richard put forward the more familiar qualities of divine love–a plurality of persons, a perfect equality of worth, and a total sharing of divine attributes–he stressed another less familiar, but crucial quality. In divine life, it is impossible for two not to be united to a third, since "sharing of love cannot exist among less than three persons" (Bk. III, Ch. 14). It seems that Richard coined a word to designate the necessity of this "third" in perfect mutual love: his term *condelictus* means one who shares in love for a third. Translator Grover Zinn considers this word crucial for reading the Victorine's theology of the Trinity and for penetrating his grasp of charity.[16] In imperfect forms of mutual love there may be affection, great longing, a "going out" to one another, but this is not the fullness of love. In the Trinity, when any one person is considered, "the other two love the third concordantly" (Bk. III, Ch. 20).

Risking mockery, Richard held the mirror of reason to Jesus' revelation concerning trinitarian love, and saw with such profundity that Ewert Cousins can describe his insights as "still seminal and open." I maintain that a certain fullness of time has arrived for receiving his understanding of mutual love in God, and what it invites. How might this fullness of mutuality be imaged within a marriage, a parish, the universal church? This question must persist throughout any contemporary exploration of the meaning of mutuality. Like any seminal thinker, Richard did not solve all the difficulties raised by his work. He has been criticized for blurring the horizon between faith and reason and for using human experience as a criterion for understanding the inner life of God. These criticisms seem to imply that faith, reason and experience should not compenetrate organically.[17]

Centuries before the west's fascination with personal self-realization, the Victorine taught that the deepest human fulfillment comes not from self-love but from transcendent love for another, from desiring "that another be loved equally by the one whom you love supremely and by whom you are supremely loved." He knew that this was rare and magnificent, and presumed persons who were capable of giving and receiving, and who would not be threatened by the gifts of others. What he attempted was "to get beneath the surface of isolation and separation to the spiritual depth where persons are intimately united at the core of their being."[18] Some contemporary theologians, especially those seeking to develop social models of the Trinity, have found Richard's insights helpful. Still others have turned to "process thought" to explain how all things, divine and human, are interrelated.

Process: The Search for the Ultimate

It may seem strange to refer to process thought in this reflection on trinitarian relations and mutuality. In fact, Jürgen Moltmann has said that process theology is inadequate for conveying Christian thought "precisely because it lacks the trinitarian perspective."[19] Why consider it, then, in this reflection on trinitarian mutuality? Several reasons prompt this attention: 1) serious theologians have attempted to reconcile the insights of process thought with trinitarian doctrine; 2) process thinkers have devised terms and categories which attempt to describe dynamic interchanges between divine persons and creation; and 3) they have sought to redefine what constitutes the very basis of all reality. The search to understand mutuality at greater depths also touches upon each of these areas, so it must be asked whether process theology is adequate for conveying the Christian understanding of divine relations and mutuality.

The writings of Alfred North Whitehead (1861–1947) serve as a common wellspring for many varieties of process thought. Whitehead was a philosopher and mathematician who construed a new understanding of reality. He saw the *entire* temporal process as a becoming, a transition from one event to another.[20] He coined the term "actual entities" to indicate the fleeting "events" or "acts" of becoming which constitute all that exists. In his view, all of reality is constituted by "actual entities" that start to perish as soon as they come into being.[21] This process can be likened to a motion picture in which distinct frames *seem* to form a constant flow. James Spiceland explains:

> The sorts of things that we might call individuals, i.e., things that endure through time, are not the real individuals, but are "societies" of these momentary experiences. Personal human existence, for instance, is a serially ordered society of occasions of experience.... At the deepest level, even these actual entities which constitute the temporal process are themselves processes, the processes of their own individual becoming.[22]

Whitehead held that God was no exception to this process, but was rather its "chief exemplification." His God was dipolar rather than trinitarian, having a "mental pole" containing all possibility, and a "physical pole" integrated with it, but derived from divine physical experience in the temporal world. Although everlasting, fully actual and conscious, this "physical pole" is determined, incomplete and consequent. This would mean that God, as well as creation, is in constant flux.[23]

Theologians working in the process stream of thought have attempted to express divine reality in more adequate terms while remaining faithful to Whitehead's interpretation. From the process perspective, there is the desire to integrate in *one continuous process* the totality of the material and the spiritual; the fleeting and the transcendent; the divine and the human. Process theologians try, as it were, to find a "field theory" that will account for both God and creation. In an age that is coming to appreciate the interrelatedness of all that exists, this theory can prove very attractive. That is why it is important to ask whether process thought genuinely accounts for trinitarian faith and whether it has valid contributions to make toward a fuller understanding of mutuality.

Within the Roman Catholic tradition, Joseph Bracken has made a concerted effort to formulate a cohesive systematic theology based in process thought. In the introduction to his book, *The Triune Symbol: Persons, Process and Community,* he says that he must begin by identifying the basic metaphysical construct which coordinates his entire system: "In brief, *it is the idea that Process, not Substance (as in scholastic philosophy), is the first category of Being or Existence.*"[24] [italics mine] This is a radical shift. In moving toward a renewed understanding of trinitarian life and mutuality, however, I suggest that neither substance nor process is adequate for designating the first category of being. As will be seen later, a more radical basis is to be found in the personal realm of *gift.* Bracken modified Whitehead's notion of God, choosing to describe the Trinity as "a structured society of three subsocieties."[25] In Bracken's frame of reference, each of the "three" is a society of entities or "occasions" rapidly succeeding one another to produce a unified divine person. Together the divine three form a genuine ontological unity "over and above the reality of its parts taken separately."[26] As the necessary principle of unity for creation, these constantly-becoming divine persons incorporate the entire world process into their communitarian life. Creation is then perceived to be part of the life-flow among the divine persons. Bracken wants to make it clear that he is proposing a form of "panentheism," rather than "pantheism." In his system, the interpersonal process in God somehow incorporates all subordinate creaturely processes without destroying their integrity. He claims that the world process, taken as a whole, is "only a part of the infinite reality of the divine Son."[27]

While Bracken asserts repeatedly that his new formulation of systematic theology is consistent with Whitehead's philosophical principles, the question remains: are these principles adequate for expressing Christian faith in the Trinity and God-creature relations? For Whitehead, *process* was the ultimate reality, a reality constituted in flux, with God involved in the same process as creatures, always in the state of becoming. William Hill says that process theologies, without exception, view the Trinity as a divine dimension "to a necessary cosmic process between God and the world. The resistance to this in mainstream Catholic thought is on the grounds that it makes process itself (Whitehead's Creativity) ultimate, rather than God."[28]

Joseph Bracken set out to reinterpret the articles of Christian belief in light of his hypothesis that being is intrinsically social and processive, and that all individual entities (including God) exist as part of still more comprehensive social entities.

Is Process Theology Adequate for the Task of Exploring Mutuality?

Despite Bracken's ground-breaking work, his system presents several difficulties: 1) there is a lack of distinction between divine community process and the multitudinous levels of process within creation; 2) this lack of distinction touches upon the person of Christ, with Bracken suggesting that the Council of Chalcedon's definition might be amended to read, "Jesus as a divine person subsists in two processes, the divine and the human";[29] and 3) process is considered the "first category of Being or Existence." Each of these is problematic, even though Bracken would view community as the highest form of process:

> In brief, I believe that reality–and by reality I mean the reality of God as well as of creation–is processive, and that community is the highest form of process, since it apparently constitutes the life of God, i.e., the three divine persons, in addition to the life of their rational creatures.... A community then is not a supraindividual person, as some have thought, but a process.[30]

Is such an interpretation of basic reality adequate in light of the last discourse? This (and not a comprehensive critique of a new synthesis) is what concerns us here. I suggest that process theories are inadequate: there is a more radical *Reality* that spurs the marvelous and complex interchanges in creation. If that were not so, process would simply be organized interchange for its own sake. Or, as Anthony Kelly observes, if God is subsumed within it, would it be more fitting to worship *process* rather than the God of Christianity?[31] Such questioning is crucial in this post-conciliar period when those who are initiating new forms of Christian community seek theological insights into the mystery of divine personal communion. The *Constitution on the Church* from the Second Vatican Council recognizes the trinitarian-centeredness of the church, says Bruno Forte: the church both comes from the Trinity and goes toward the Trinity.[32] It is the *meaning and character* of the divine personal communion that must be received more deeply before its image in the church can be genuinely received also. Over five hundred years ago the Council of Florence reaffirmed belief in God's inner unity:

> On account of this unity the Father is wholly in the Son, and wholly in the Holy Spirit; the Son wholly in the Father and wholly in the Holy Spirit; the Holy Spirit wholly in the Father and wholly in the Son. None precedes the other in eternity, none exceeds in greatness, nor excels in power.[33]

The Trinity: Perichoretic Love

If it is true that a certain "fullness of time" has come for understanding divine mutual love, there will be a new capacity to ponder what it means to "live wholly within one another" not simply as a "process" but as realization of interpersonal communion. Jesus' prayer at the last supper, asking that his followers participate in divine unity, is like a persistent knock on the door of human receptivity, awaiting response. "Living wholly within one another" is not only a medieval assertion about divine life, but also applies to Jesus' prayer "that they may be one as we are one." In order to be opened to the realization of that prayer, it is necessary to know in some connatural manner what this means for the Father, Son and Holy Spirit. Here the terms *perichoresis* and *circuminsession,* introduced earlier, invite further reflection. Since the Greek word *perichoresis* bears a double meaning, two closely-related Latin terms are needed to express it equivalently. Leonardo Boff explains this well:

> Theology came to use the Greek word *perichoresis* to express this interpenetration of one Person by the others.... Its first meaning is that of one being contained in another, dwelling in, being in another—a situation of fact, a static state. This understanding was translated by *circuminsessio,* a word derived from *sedere* and *sessio,* being seated, having its seat in, seat. Applied to the mystery of the communion of the Trinity this signified: one Person is in the others, surrounds the others on all sides (*circum-*), occupies the same space as the others, fills them with its presence. Its second meaning is active and signifies the interpenetration or

> interweaving of one Person with the others and in the others. This understanding seeks to express the living and eternal process of relating intrinsic to the three Persons, so that each is always penetrating the others. This meaning was translated as *circumincessio,* derived from *incedere,* meaning to permeate, com-penetrate and interpenetrate.[34]

These terms convey the twofold expression of divine union: interpenetrating activity, and enduring presence to one another. *Divine communion means the capacity to go out and to remain at the same "time."* Each person is necessarily within the other two, and yet is simultaneously an irresistible outward impulse into the other two. There is an "unceasing circulation of life."[35] Long before the twentieth century penchant for motion and process, Cyril of Alexandria described trinitarian relations as "reciprocal irruption [sic]" (PG 73:81). English words suggesting perichoretic union are "dancing about," "encompassing," "coinhering," and "interpenetrating."[36]

Christian Art and Perichoretic Love

How do these words take flesh in the contemporary church? How does the possibility of entering into perichoretic union become the very way of life within marriages and local faith communities? The memory of the church is not only transmitted through its rich verbal tradition, but also through its visual/tactile theological heritage. Despite centuries of war and violent destruction, there remains an enduring inheritance of artistic works, sacred music and architecture to be received anew by each generation, allowing a bodily sharing in the lived faith of earlier Christians. Any authentic new "leap" in the understanding of trinitarian life and mutuality will result in a keener sensitivity to the manner in which these mysteries of relationship have already been experienced in the church. The frescos, mosaics and sculpted figures of the ancient basilicas and gothic cathedrals hold this Christian memory.

Of the numerous examples in the city of Rome, I cite only two: St. Clement's and the basilica St. Mary in Trestevere. In each, the twofold mystery of dynamic process and enduring union is limned in the mosaic floor patterns that swirl toward the eucharistic altar, one circle caught up in the other. The tree of life mosaic in the apse of St.

Clement's is a consummate example of unitive design. On the long facade of St. Mary, ten virgins *process* toward the virgin nursing her child, and the portico walls are embedded with puteal fragments depicting fruitful vines and joined circles.

In some cathedrals large circles mark a time when ring dances were incorporated into the celebration of major feasts. Large stone labyrinths transformed ancient legends about death and burial into signs of resurrection, with Christ or the church signified at the center.[37] Together these places of worship serve as a compendium of theological insight and common faith. Since art and architecture reflect inner perceptions and the theological emphases of different periods, it is perhaps useful to observe the unsettled state of current church art and architecture.

Both new and remodeled church buildings of the late twentieth century bear the record of post-conciliar struggles to understand divine-human relationships and the meaning of community. The semicircular design of many new structures invites a union about the altar, but the near-barren walls and individual banners are often at variance with the contemporary emphasis upon body-person, community and Trinity. Sometimes venerable old places of worship present an awkward or disjointed appearance as congregations rearrange altars, baptismal fonts and choir areas to foster a communal celebration. Church art is reflecting our often uneasy attempts to reconcile individual fulfillment with interpersonal communion. As will be seen later, it is striking that the communities presented in this work as examples of lived mutuality have consciously sought to express their experience through artistic and architectural media: the Black Christ in Ceciliaville, the icons in the church of St. Egidio, and the multiple unitive expressions in glass and stone at the Abbey of Regina Laudis.

Although many contemporary churches in the west are almost severe in their lack of artistic representation of the faith, the so-called "icon of the Trinity" by the fifteenth century monk, Paisij, retains a universal appeal. The icon depicts three sacral figures grouped about a table. They are sometimes thought to represent either the three mysterious visitors to Abraham and Sarah or the moment of revelation at the Emmaus meal–or the three divine persons. The "wings" of the three, almost imperceptible at first, touch and convey intimacy. An anonymous commentator notes how the three at table form a circle, "symbol of the bread and the chalice which contains a calf's head (symbol of the lamb of sacrifice) which becomes the center of the circle outlined by the angels' figures. The zenith of this communion of the Trinity is, consequently, God's love for man, this Eternal Counsel of the Incarnation."[38] The writer notes how the icon opens to those who gaze upon it, drawing them from a temporal to an eternal dimension. There is no definitive interpretation of the figures' identities, no surety about Paisij's intent to portray divine persons.

Possibly, the figure to the right depicts the Father, behind whom rises a mountain, symbol of grandeur. The figure to his right may depict the Son, behind whom is the tree of life. To the left may be the symbolic figure of the Holy Spirit, behind whom rises a church. The icon conveys both intimacy and elusive mystery. The three comprise an open circle, receptive to those who contemplate them.

Perhaps the contrast between a) appreciation for the trinitarian icon, and b) the desire for artistic severity in current church design, reflects a deeper tension within the body of believers. Inner-faith conviction cannot long be dissociated from appropriate language and visual/tactile expressions without becoming merely cerebral, or worse, irrelevant. Brian Hebblethwaite notes how the poet W. H. Auden used the trinitarian term *perichoresis* with great effect in his poem "Compline," and comments:

> It is a striking fact that the technical theological term "perichoresis" can appear with such effect in a modern poem.... How strange, then, that in theology itself, such words [as *perichoresis*] have lost their power! Not only has the Christian mind in general ceased to register the significance of the technical terms of orthodox trinitarian theology but many theologians themselves now recommend us to jettison such terms, and indeed the doctrine of the Trinity itself, as part of the outworn lumber of the Christian past. Thus Professor Wiles writes in his essay in *Christian Believing:* "I cannot with integrity say that I believe God to be one in three persons."[39]

For many in the post-modern, post-conciliar west, the Trinity and perichoretic unity seem unreal, removed from reasonableness and daily life. Hebblethwaite's observations add urgency to the questions: what does it *mean* that the three divine persons relate perichoretically, and what does it mean for us? In the context of the last discourse, what does Jesus *mean* in saying, "You must believe me when I say that I am in the Father and the Father is in me" (Jn 14:11) and "I shall ask the Father and he will give you another Advocate.... but you know him, because he is with you, he is in you" (Jn 14:16, 17)? While Jesus' revelation was given personally and in personal terms, theological references to inner trinitarian life are often abstract, lacking the whole-person-involving dynamic which inspired the whorled mosaics reeling toward the apse of St. Clement's basilica and the fifteenth century icon of the Trinity.

Human Imaging of the Three-Personal God

I think that Richard Schneider touched the nub of the problem in a pivotal lecture, "The Human Person as Image of the Three-Personal God." Generally, he said, Christians have tended to interpret Genesis 1:26 ("Let us make man in our own image, in the likeness of ourselves") to mean that the human person is made in the image of the divine *nature*. The weakness in this interpretation lies in seeing human *nature* as the image of divine *nature* (the human intellect and will reflecting God's willing and knowing). While this is not incorrect, said Schneider, "it is rather incomplete because the emphasis should be on person rather than on nature. The human person is the image of the divine person."[40] Pagan antiquity did not have a developed notion of person: this formed and developed within the Christian tradition as a "by-product" of theological reflection on the mysteries of Trinity and incarnation. In Christianity there was a development from emphasis on the *substance* character of person to an emphasis on the *relational* character of person. Every person has both immanence and transcendence. Personal immanence means individuality: there is an incommunicable depth which makes one person intrinsically different from all others. Transcendence, on the other hand, refers to relatedness–an openness to God, other persons, and all of creation. There is a close link between immanence and transcendence since it is only by transcending self that a person attains personal immanence. While the perfection of this is impossible for human beings, it is precisely what Christ revealed concerning the inner life of God. Schneider described the interflow of divine life:

> The First Person is the complete giving of the divine essence through generation and spiration.... His very existence and identity depend upon this two-fold relation.... The Son, the Second Person of the Trinity, is the acceptance of the divine essence and is the active giving (together with the Father) of the divine essence to the Spirit. His immanence consists in his relation of Sonship and active Spiration.... The immanence of the Spirit consists in his transcendence to the Father and the Son, in his active acceptance of the divine nature from the Father.... We have here an explanation of the revelation of a perfect community of persons. The three divine persons are persons by being related to one another.... In God the persons are constituted by the dynamic mutual giving of themselves.[41]

Donum Theology: A Theology of Gift

To be human is to be created in the image of God and the call to human mutuality can be recognized in the divine paradigm where 1) the *identity* of each divine person is in *relation* to the other two; 2) their perfect mutual love requires a *third*; 3) their reciprocal love is an *indwelling;* and 4) the basis of their interrelationship is *personal self-gift.* It is important now to focus on the fourth aspect of divine mutuality: personal self-gift.

Jesus spoke of his own mission, and that of the Holy Spirit in terms of gift and he revealed the Father as one who sends person-gifts. In the eucharistic canon, the paschal mystery is celebrated in the context of gifts given and received:

> Take this, all of you, and eat it: this is my body which will be given up for you.... Take this all of you, and drink from it: this is the cup of my blood, the blood of the new and everlasting covenant. It will be shed for you and for all so that sins may be forgiven.... Do this in memory of me.

Gifts of bread and wine are brought to this consummate transformation and the third eucharistic prayer asks in the name of the community, "May he make us an everlasting gift to you." Long before the last supper Jesus had prepared the disciples for his own permanent self-gift. When the Samaritan woman was distracted by water buckets and Jacob's status, Jesus began to speak to her of *gift:* "If only you knew what God is offering and who it is that is saying to you: "Give me to drink," you would have been the one to ask, and he would have given you living water.... The water that I shall give will turn into a spring inside, welling up to eternal life" (Jn 4:10,14). When crowds pursued Jesus after the multiplication of loaves and fishes, he spoke again of person-gift. He identified himself as the living bread, saying, "The bread that I shall give is my flesh for the life of the world" (Jn 6:51).

The witness of the New Testament is that Jesus and the Holy Spirit are sent into human history as gifts who would literally enter into those who received them and abide with them. What is characteristic of this immanent life of God is also true of trinitarian actions which accomplished human salvation, or as Karl Rahner and Herbert Vorgrimler have it: "the Trinity of God's dealings with us is already the reality of God as he is in himself: tri-'personality.'"[42] In God, love is total gift, but it is especially to the Holy Spirit that the name "gift" is attributed. Pope John Paul II writes:

> It can be said that in the Holy Spirit the intimate life of the Triune God becomes totally gift, an exchange of mutual love between the divine Persons, and that through the Holy Spirit God exists in the mode of gift. It is the Holy Spirit who is the *personal expression* of this self-giving, this being-love. He is Person-Love. He is Person-Gift.[43]

Yet it is precisely because Father and Son are themselves poured out as gift that the Holy Spirit–complete receptivity and response in turn–is known as gift. The basis of trinitarian relations, and thus the source of divine personal identity is self-gift. It is the Holy Spirit from whom "derives as from its source.... *all giving of gifts* vis-à-vis creatures."[44] The theology of mutuality is then a *Donum* theology, or a theology of gift.

Can one say more–that gift is the ultimate basis of all reality? Neither substance nor process is adequate for expressing that which is foundational for all being. As Schneider noted, we have developed beyond the point of understanding divine persons primarily in terms of *substance*. In *perichoresis* there is a mutual indwelling, an abiding personal "content" which cannot adequately be described in terms of process. The dynamism of process is for the sake of person-gifts, given and received equally and in deference to one another. This has profound implications for a theology intended to ground a spirituality of interpersonal relations.

Many theologians are searching for categories that are adequate to express new insights, that can accommodate shifts in terminology. I propose that the initial grounding point for understanding all reality is neither substance nor process, but *gift*. Rather than dismissing all that has been signified by the scholastic term substance, or opting for process as the ultimate reality, I see *gift* as illuminating and uniting both. The understanding of *gift* springs from Christian revelation, but it is also applicable across various philosophical systems. Theologically, *gift* expresses not only the inner life of God from which all reality springs, but also creation and redemption. It also names the human vocation to be the image of God, the enfleshed analogy of divine love.

It is helpful to see how the qualities of authentic human gift-giving shed light on this. Gifts are love-impelled and they mark relationships. They are given freely, not out of necessity. Gifts are proffered and received without calculation or self-benefit. In human gifting, the tangible gift is an extension of the whole person, denoting in some limited way, "I give myself to you." Carefully chosen gifts represent thought, the sacrifice of time and resources in order to select that which expresses most suitably the relationship being celebrated. *The more closely a gift conveys the giver's person and presence, the more perfect the gift. Nothing can replace the actual person, given in some appropriate manner.* When a beloved overcomes great obstacles or bears supreme cost to be personally present as *the* gift, both self-realization and communion attain great perfection. In trinitarian love, divine persons are unceasingly sharing in total self-giving and receiving. John O'Donnell writes of the vocation to be image of this communion:

> From a theological perspective the deepest reason for the human being's sociality is that the person is created in the image of the Trinity, the perfect community, where the three divine persons exist in an eternal self-giving. *Gaudium et Spes* hinted at this truth when it affirmed that there is such a likeness between the divine community and the human community that the human person is precisely that

> being who can realize himself only by giving himself away. The Council Fathers wrote: "man, who is the only creature on earth which God willed for itself, cannot fully find himself except through a sincere gift of himself."[45] (#24,2)

The mutuality of divine self-gift is so radical that it means "wholly living within one another." It must now be asked how this opens to human participation at the present time. In his farewell, Jesus prayed that his disciples might also "live within one another." In order to penetrate more deeply into this mystery it is necessary to probe the *human* participative meaning of mutuality.

CHAPTER THREE

The Human Search for Mutuality

> In loving another, we become a gifted presence to that person. We wish to live in union (the true meaning of "communion") with that person so as to be present as often as possible, not only physically in space and time, but more importantly in the inner recesses of our consciousness. We are this way because God is this way in His essence as Love.
>
> –*George A. Maloney*[1]

There is an explicit *human vocation* to be the image of divine mutual love and every creaturely manifestation of it will bear trinitarian "vestiges." While deriving from the divine communion, creaturely mutuality remains partial, and will always lack the divine completeness. This causes an inexpressible loneliness at the core of personal life, expressed in the familiar prayer of St. Augustine: "Our hearts are made for you, O Lord, and they are restless until they rest in you." Where human mutuality is genuine, however, the characteristics of divine perichoresis will be reflected. That is, personal identity will be realized in faithful relationships; there will be reciprocal giving and receiving among equals; and there will be an openness to "thirds." What remains still quite unexplored is the manner in which perichoresis–mutual indwelling–is actualized within the people of God. In living out these qualities of mutual love, the community of faith becomes a "sacrament" of divine mutuality in the world. It is at once the community's privilege and terrible vulnerability: becoming total gift. At times this also requires the loving capacity to reconcile what at first seems incompatible, echoing Gabriel's words, "for nothing is impossible to God." Theological exploration of these qualities of human mutuality is greatly assisted today by insights from other disciplines, as varied as they may be. The writings of Martin Buber and scientific data concerning perichoretic patterns in the universe are particularly helpful here. And everywhere, from the basic doctrines of faith to the behavior of subatomic particles, there is need to reconcile the incongruous!

Perhaps no other in this century has addressed *human* mutuality with greater directness and contemplative care than the Jewish philosopher Martin Buber. While he did not reflect from a trinitarian perspective, his spare, profound assertions about I-You relationships contribute greatly to understanding 1) the basic attitude required for mutual relations; and 2) the varying levels on which mutuality can be lived. In *I and Thou* Buber said there are two possible attitudes or two "basic words" that characterize our meetings with an "other." These basic words are I-You and I-It.

> When one says You, the I of the word pair I-You is said, too. When one says It, the I of the word pair I-It is said, too. The basic word I-You can only be spoken with one's whole being. The basic word I-It can never be spoken with one's whole being.[2]

In these few sentences Buber summarized the two fundamental attitudes toward all that exists. His two basic words resonate with Arthur Gibson's distinctions between essentialist and existentialist thought. When a person relates to an other as a "You," said Buber, the other is not simply an object: "When You is said there is no something. You has no borders. Whoever says You does not have something; he has nothing. But he stands in relation."[3] For Buber, this is very different from simply *experiencing* another since "experience" happens only to the one experiencing. It does no good to modify the word experience with adjectives like "mysterious" or "inner." Buber says wryly of such attempts: "O mysteriousness without mystery, O piling up of information! It, it, it!"[4] Experience belongs to the I-It realm, while relation belongs to the I-You realm. He considered the word *encounter* to be the appropriate term for expressing an I-You relation since it signifies an act done with one's whole being, requiring sacrifice and risk. There is a mystical quality in Buber's saying:

> When I confront a human being as my You and speak the basic word I-You to him, then he is no thing among things

> nor does he consist of things.... Neighborless and seamless, he is You and fills the firmament. Not as if there were nothing but he; but everything else lives in *his* light.[5]

This basic attitude is not limited to the personal realm. *Every* being is to be encountered as a "You"; but this is possible only when the basic I-You attitude permeates one's entire being. Then reciprocity is possible whether the encounter is with another human being, a tree or a star.

Degrees of Mutuality

Buber's saying that there are different levels of mutuality has troubled some of his readers who think that he blurred necessary distinctions between personal and nonpersonal beings. As Donald Berry explains, it was a matter of remaining faithful to the actuality of the *encounter* while acknowledging the "difference that being non-human makes."[6] Every meeting, with persons as well as with animals and inanimate creatures, is either relational (I-You) or objective (I-It). Since this is the living out of a basic attitude, it pervades the person and cannot be worn like a coat or selected for specific occasions. In Anton Pegis' words, there is a search in the late twentieth century for a theology of humanity in which "spiritual union with matter, beginning with the matter of.... body and extending across the earth toward outer space, is the central and paramount reality."[7] Such reciprocity is not easily attained. Because he recognized the varying levels of mutuality and their incompleteness, Buber could move beyond sentimental notions of giving and receiving: "Everything tells you that complete mutuality does not inhere in men's life with one another. It is a form of grace for which one must always be prepared but on which one can never count."[8]

Some of Buber's richest insights regarding mutuality come in the "Afterword" to *I and Thou,* written forty years after the original text. In it he addressed anew the levels or spheres of mutuality. For example, he described what it means to "tame" animals, noting how they can detect feigned tenderness. Those most able to form "partnership" with animals "are by no means 'animalistic' by nature but rather spiritual."[9] He named the I-You encounter with animals the "threshold of mutuality."[10]

For beings that lack the spontaneity of humans and animals, Buber needed a further distinction. This immense range of beings, from plants to stones and stars, form the "pre-threshold of mutuality." Difficulties in perceiving a level of mutuality on the pre-threshold level lie in human unawareness. The contemplative philosopher Buber alleged that where there is an openness to nonpersonal beings, "something is awakened by our attitude and flashes toward us from that which has being."[11] As will be shown in later chapters, this reality is clearly understood by the Benedictine nuns of Regina Laudis in their relation to the land, and by the Sponsor Couples Community who see their workplace as the locus of encounter and cocreativity. It is not a question of analysis, said Buber. That makes one a mere investigator. Oaks and black holes and metal-stamping machines will be manifest in their being to one who approaches them with a mutuality of presence. Beyond the personal, threshold and pre-threshold levels of mutuality there is the level of spiritual encounter, which Buber called the "over-threshold," meaning literally "the lintel over the door." Even this realm requires division into two spheres. First, in daily existence there are spiritual forms which are as real as material ones. Second, there is that elusive spiritual realm which Buber described as "not having entered the world," and to which he really could not point:

> If I am asked here, too, in the case of this borderland, where one is supposed to find mutuality, I can only point indirectly to certain scarcely describable events in human life where spirit was encountered; and if this indirect procedure proves inadequate, nothing remains to me in the end but an appeal to the testimony of your own mysteries, my reader, which may be buried under debris but are presumably still accessible to you.[12]

Buber said that while human relationship with God cannot be fully mutual, it is the universal relation "into which all rivers pour without drying up for that reason."[13] In relationship with God (whom Buber considered absolute person) human beings do not receive "content" but presence and strength. Although he did not write from a trinitarian perspective, he found that divine presence and strength included three elements "that are not separate but may nevertheless be contemplated as three."[14] First, being admitted into the divine presence makes life meaningful. Second, it confirms a meaning that is beyond formulas and images: "Nothing, nothing can henceforth be meaningless."[15] Third, this meaning applies to the present life where it can be received and put into action. Buber concluded his Afterword thus: "The existence of mutuality between God and man cannot be proved any more than the existence of God. Anyone who dares nevertheless to speak of it bears witness and invokes the witness of those whom he addresses–present or future witness."[16]

In the course of explaining what he meant by I-You and I-It relations, Buber also named what he considered the basic category of existence. It was neither substance nor process; it was relation: "In the beginning is the relation–as the category of being, as readiness, as a form that reaches out to be filled, as a model of the soul; the *a priori* of relation; *the innate You*."[17] Perhaps his lack of connaturality with a trinitarian understanding of God explains why he did not move beyond *relation* itself to that which underlies divine relations: person-gift.

Buber did not sentimentalize the meaning of relation, and he appreciated the limits present in all human forms of mutuality. Some relations, by their very nature, place normative limits; for example those between teacher and student; psychotherapist and client; spiritual leader and disciple. The enabling person in each case must simultaneously be at both poles of a bipolar relationship–one's own unique pole and the other's pole (where the effects of one's actions are internalized). Although he was not contemplating mutuality from a Christian trinitarian perspective, Martin Buber voiced the twentieth century readiness for deeper union.

Triads in Human Experience

In recent decades disciplines such as physics, architecture, music and the visual arts have emphasized the beauty and synergistic potential of triads, awakening appreciation for the "three's" that abound in daily experience. Examples of what have traditionally been called "vestiges" of the Trinity are found everywhere in creation. Earthly existence unfolds within the three dimensions of height, length and depth. Water serves the human family as liquid, vapor and ice (each form sharing the same "substantial reality" but manifesting unique, seemingly contradictory qualities). Under the influence of temperature, the same substance can either allow an airplane to slip through its cloudy translucence, or it can support that same plane on the surface of a frozen lake. Seed, flowering plant and mature fruit participate in the same life continuum. Everywhere in nature, there are hints of the mystery of divine mutual indwelling–the simultaneous remaining within, yet going out.

The lived human body is a compendium of triads, many of which are based on receptivity, response, and a fruitful "third." The ear, for example, actively receives the spoken word and from this interaction comes thought (or image, or answering word). Nostrils welcome fragrances which, in turn, evoke memory, delight or disgust. Of course, procreative union is paradigmatic. For that reason alone, the mystery of three-in-one should prove a most familiar pattern. Within the intimacy of married, life-giving love there is (even if ever so briefly) a form of "living within one another." From the union of parental gifts rises the spiraling dance of a unique genetic design that permanently marks the child conceived, the vital third of their love.

This is not to suggest that all triunities are positive and life-giving in a sin-wounded world. There are destructive triads which not only eliminate a "third" but also endanger others beyond them. These are I-It forms of interaction in which there is a taking or a being-taken, in which there are power struggles and the seeking of personal advantage at the expense of others. In these situations, a "third" can become a pawn or be objectified for pleasure, status or material gain. Philosopher Jean-Paul Sartre considered this a normal state of affairs. In *Being and Nothingness* he dwelt on what it means to be living bodily in the hostile world. Like Buber, Jean-Paul Sartre spoke of two basic attitudes in meeting an "other." In his case, both were nonrelational. One either acknowledged having been made an "object" by an other (causing shame) or affirmed self-freedom, making the *other* into an object (causing pride).[18] In neither case could there be a real encounter, much less any mutuality. In his famous description of "the stare," Sartre asserted that merely to be "looked at" meant a loss of one's powers; it was a form of subordination:

> The look which the eyes manifest, no matter what kind of eyes they are, is a pure reference to myself. What I apprehend immediately when I hear the branches crackling behind me is not that *there is someone there;* it is that I am

> vulnerable, that I have a body which can be hurt, that I occupy a place and that I can not in any case escape from the space in which I am without defense–in short, that I *am seen.* Thus the look is first an intermediary which refers from me to myself.[19]

It would be difficult to find a more consummate example of negative individualism, closed to any possibility of mutuality. For Sartre, the body was a terrible liability since it made the human being completely vulnerable. "A dull and inescapable nausea perpetually reveals my body to my consciousness,"[20] he wrote. Within Sartre's perspective, every human interaction became a threat rather than the possibility of giving and receiving.

Certainly daily life is punctuated by multiple instances of wounded or destructive triads, and the lived body is always vulnerable. The gospels provide classic examples. Jesus' enemies utilized a variety of "thirds" to entrap him: legal prescriptions, persons in need of physical healing, and a woman accused of adultery. Psychotherapist Harriet Lerner shows how (even unconsciously) spouses and others in close association use "thirds" in order to detour responsibility for their basic problems.[21] By no means are all three-in-one's in daily life positive, witnessing to perichoretic love.

Nevertheless, on all levels of existence, dynamic interchange is a hallmark of the universe. There is an amazing perichoretic patterning at work in the unseen micro-levels of created matter–a "living within one another" of seemingly unrelated beings, a nonpersonal giving and receiving which may seem random, but which increasingly is known to possess a high degree of order. Aaron Wasserman says almost casually in his college text, *Biology,* that electrons are not confined to an orbital area: "[T]here is a small but statistically measurable possibility that an electron or atom in this book is somewhere out in the Milky Way. Orbitals describe probabilities, not certainties."[22]

We have become accustomed to speaking of the smallest elements of micro-matter as "sometimes-particle, sometimes-wavicle" in behavior. David Freedman, reporting on recent research into subatomic particles, says: "If you've grown comfortable with particles being in two places at once, dissolving into waves when no one is looking, and communicating faster than the speed of light, then these latest experiments in quantum mechanics won't bother you at all."[23] The more precise their instruments have become, the more researchers find that the seemingly "objective" study of particles is really an interaction. Even "looking at" the transition from wave to particle makes a difference in the activity of subatomic beings. Human bodies, magnolias, fence posts and space vehicles are in a whirling interchange that transcends the earth and its near neighbors.

After his return from the moon mission, Captain James Irwin described the intense, sometimes inexplicable communications that he had known while working on the lunar surface. On one occasion he was preparing a science station at some distance from the Lunar Module and a key string broke. Irwin prayed since the immediate answer that he needed could not wait upon an answer from Houston. He claimed that he had a supernatural sense of divine presence and received immediate direction. "We all thought with a new clarity, almost a clairvoyance," he said. "I could almost anticipate what Dave Scott was going to say, and I felt that I knew what he was thinking."[24] After the journey was over, the moon became a creative "third" for Irwin:

> Indirectly, everyone on earth was a part of this flight. It was a human effort.... I feel the responsibility of being a representative.... Everybody wants to talk to a man who has been to the moon. They think that since he has seen something they have not seen and will never see, he must know something they do not know.... They are interested in what happened inside us, in our hearts and souls. They can't go to the moon, but they can take this flight.... The moon has a powerful force; it seems to affect the feelings and behavior of everybody. I cannot imagine a holier place.[25]

Captain Irwin spoke of the moon voyage in terms of what he had received and what he felt impelled to give; the reciprocity he knew with the moon was rooted in his interpersonal relations with God and "everyone on earth." Insights from all disciplines which search for truth about the human body and the universe of material beings are extremely helpful in the ongoing quest to understand mutuality. As early as the fifth century, Cyril of Alexandria in a commentary on John's gospel (PG 74, 553–61) asserted that Christians know a relationship of love and concord with divine persons by communing in the sacred body of Christ and having fellowship with the Holy Spirit. He added boldly: *this is a real, physical union.*[26] Scientific research is providing valuable insights into the physical universe at the very time when faith communities are searching for a deepened understanding of perichoretic union. There is a coinherence among the mysteries of faith, and that is imaged in the compenetration of divine and human, spiritual and material in Jesus Christ.

Mystery and Gift

What Martin Buber called the "over-threshold" of mutuality, Christians know as encounter with divine mystery. Karl Rahner observed that mystery is so closely interwoven with the ordinary that it can easily be missed or misinterpreted. Or, as he put it, mystery "does not need to be fetched" since it is "the impenetrable which is already present."[27] In order to express this awareness it is sometimes more helpful to rely on poetry or narrative rather than the whitened bones of technical language. Poet Sister Maura Eichner muses that we "walk in miracles as children scuff through daisy fields" and of her own lived body with its union of matter and spirit, its summation of parental gifts, she wrote in *What We Women Know:*

> Under my breastbone
> I can almost touch the home-made
> mobile that my father with
> my mother made.
> Someone
> is there–signing my own
> legend with a cross.

All Christian mysteries derive from the core mystery of divine mutual love and every human person is invited to participate in that divine communion which is realized through self-gift. All lesser gifts of relationship and compenetration within the universe are to be received in light of it. This can seem a remote ideal, but in the simplicity of the gospels, one finds that it characterized the life of Jesus as he ate, labored, taught and suffered. He continually extended relationships into life-giving "thirds." Whatever another offered by way of need or gift, he brought to new possibility. *The potential for extraordinary exchange resided in the ordinary.* A young boy's gift of barley loaves and fishes was received and transformed so that the multitude was nourished. Those who brought the gift of faith received in turn, the "third" of health, or even the restoration of their loved ones from the dead. Jesus saw *all* in terms of gift, from the life he shared with the Father and the Paraclete, to the field lilies lavishly spread on the Galilean hills.

Kaethe Kollwitz has said that "Every gift conceals a task."[28] Ultimately, it is the task of giving self in return. From the perfect, reciprocal giving and receiving among the divine persons comes the self-gift of Jesus Christ and the indwelling gift of the Holy Spirit, expressive of the creative self-gift of the Father. Each exists only in relation to the others, desiring and enhancing the glory of the others. Or, as Hans Urs von Balthasar said: "This means that God.... is pure selflessness, pure devotion to the loved One."[29]

I have suggested that neither "substance" nor "process" is adequate for designating the first category of being. Rather, it is *gift,* which in trinitarian relations and identity is always total person-gift. Limited and imperfect as the image of this gift will be in human persons, *the giving and receiving of gifts is the basic human vocation,* and all creation shares in appropriate ways of signing and confirming this vocation. The category of *gift* (given and received) applies across all disciplines. Scientists employ technical terms for the interchanges and fruitful activity observed in the universe, but derivatively, all are created in the mode of gift.

Although the universe has always been permeated with echoes of the Trinity, the revelation of inner divine love had to be revealed in a way that human beings could know and receive it. Divine self-gift became flesh. That is why Edward Schillebeeckx could say that Christ is "the sacrament of the encounter with God."[30] In him the effective self-gift of the Trinity became palpable. Before the enduring presence of the eucharistic blessed sacrament, there was the primordial sacrament of Jesus' lived body, processing through the streets of Nazareth, Capharnaum and Jerusalem.

In order that there might be divine-human mutuality, there had to be an awareness of the divine gift being offered. While it will take the entire span of human history to plumb at increasing depths the meaning of such gift, there was sufficient readiness within God's people at the time of the incarnation that *some* could recognize and receive the primordial sacrament of God-gift come in the flesh. Over fishing nets and in the homes of tax collectors Jesus lived out his sacramental mission of revealing the meaning of divine love, until in the paschal mystery he entered once for all into a forever-covenant with women and men who would receive him, sealing that covenant in his body and blood.

If there had been no means of continuity with the outward saving gift of Jesus, intimate human interchange with the Trinity would have been encapsulated within the brief period that he lived in the Near East. It is for that reason that the church continues to be the sacrament of Christ's living presence. The *Dogmatic Constitution on the Church* speaks of the church as "a kind of sacrament or sign of intimate union with God, and the unity of all mankind," and the "instrument" for achieving such union and unity.[31] In turn, the entire world bears a sacramental quality, prompting Nathan Wood to say that the "triunity of Father, Son and Holy Spirit which supplies the universe with its cause and explanation comes to us in Jesus.... We live in a world which is his vivid likeness, amid a universe of interwoven movement which is his seamless robe."[32] For us, mutuality is never simply a "spiritual" exchange: it must be embodied in a sacramental world.

Incongruity and Sacred Unity

One major obstacle in accepting the possibility of divine-human mutuality is simply that it seems so *incongruous* at times. That has a significance which may escape us at first, so it is helpful to dwell on it momentarily. "Incongruity" implies that there is a radical disproportion or an inherent inconsistency in the union of two (or more) realities, making the unity seem to be absurd or at least lacking in propriety.

Children expect the incongruous and delight in it. Fairy tales abound in speaking beasts, the performance of impossible tasks, and the uttering of words that are immediately effective. Fairy tales and children can overleap the obvious, making way for conversion or radical transformation. Although the tales take for granted an easy familiarity among persons, animals and the larger world, things are never quite what they first seem to be. Story and child express a longing for the apparently impossible, making it seem as common as supper that a red-suited gift-giver traverses arctic skies in an open sleigh, comes down one's very own chimney on Christmas Eve, and scatters lavish gifts under a housebound tree. There is a simultaneous anticipation of the gifts, and a longing/dread of *seeing* the giver in this wondrous act. Part of the delight is surprise: being visited in one's home by the gift-giver during the unknowingness of sleep. Edward Schillebeeckx says that "Human encounter proceeds through the visible obviousness of the body, which is a sign that reveals and at the same time veils the human interiority."[33] There lurks in the adult heart, seasoned with pain and disappointment, a hope that the impossible may happen, that the "gift-giver" will come, and that there is more than meets the eye.

Perhaps it is something of that hope which impels research in quantum physics–and gives delight when subatomic particles behave differently if "no one is looking." Humor is often based on the incongruous, on verbal or visual combinations that defy the obvious. When a humorist brings together what seemingly cannot be related, there is a burst of delight: laughter. It is a human, personal response. Crocodiles do not exchange jokes while lolling in the everglades, and no matter how long household dogs and cats are exposed to situation comedies, they will not break into laughter. Laughter is a peculiarly human response and it is closely linked to the incongruity present in impenetrable mystery. Lives of the saints (especially those written before critical methods were employed to separate fact from loving legend) have often revealed an at-homeness with the seemingly impossible and a delight in the humorous![34] Like the particles and wavicles of quantum physics, the holy and the humorous sometimes blur into one another and are forms of energy.

The scriptures provide delightful examples: a boy's slingshot pitted against a giant's armor; a diminutive tax collector shinnying down a sycamore tree; a dead man shuffling from his tomb in winding sheets. Both Abraham and Sarah laughed at the incongruity of Sarah conceiving a child at the age of ninety! When the promise was fulfilled, Sarah said, "God has given me cause to laugh; all those who hear of it will laugh with me" (Gn 21:7).

It is not surprising that holiness is linked with humor and incongruity. Christians aver that God is faithfully present even in dire circumstances, that evil will not have the last word, and that transcendent reality exceeds human calculations. The saints give witness to this: Thomas More joked with his executioner, and Teresa of Avila seasoned her mystical writings with wry observations on the incongruities of life. On the other hand, those who are convinced that human existence terminates at death feel a grim need to maintain deliberate control over persons and events that touch their lives (some see the whole life enterprise as absurd, lacking in any meaning). Then, whatever is random or unplanned becomes a threat. Christian faith in the resurrection does not involve a denial of suffering, nor does it remove the pain of rude interruptions and death. Rather it affirms that death is a *transformation,* not a meaningless termination. Earthly life and death are a participation in mystery, not an exercise in absurdity.

In Christopher Fry's *The Lady's Not for Burning,* Thomas and Jennett dialogue about death. Thomas asks, "Do we waste the evening / Commiserating with each other about / The unhygienic condition of our worm-cases? / For God's sake, shall we laugh?" When Jennett asks the reason, Thomas replies:

> For the reason of laughter, since laughter is sure
> The surest touch of genius in creation.
> Would *you* ever have thought of it, I ask you,
> If you had been making man, stuffing him full
> Of such hopping greeds and passions that he has
> To blow himself to pieces as often as he
> Conveniently can manage it—would it also
> Have occurred to you to make him burst himself
> With such a phenomenon as cachinnation?
> That same laughter, madam, is an irrelevancy
> Which almost amounts to revelation.[35]

The ability to *expect* and to *see* connections between seemingly disparate realities prepares Christians to receive the mystery of trinitarian life within a sacramental world *and to participate in various levels of mutuality.* The basic mysteries of faith are humanly incongruous: three persons in one God; two natures in the one person, Jesus Christ; the God-man born of a virgin; the crucified savior rising from the dead; and the risen Christ giving himself as food and drink. Not only are these seemingly incompatible assertions reconciled in Christian faith, they are the foundational mysteries received by the people of God—the very possibility for human fulfillment. Depth understanding of mutuality is impossible without a capacity for welcoming the incongruous. This begins with receiving the incongruous union that is the living body-person.

Mutuality Within the Human Person

In what would seem a contradiction, the human person is a union of matter and spirit. It is this union that *constitutes* the human being. This mysterious union is lived so intimately that it ordinarily escapes direct reflection until something threatens it. Skilled practitioners in medicine and the life sciences have become increasingly adept at dividing and subdividing the physical organs and functions of the person. Integration is far more difficult to foster than analysis and technical manipulation. From the moment of human conception there begins a mutuality of body and soul, of matter and spirit, that will be in fruitful tension until death. Often there are attempts to resolve this tension by reducing the person to either matter or spirit (some claiming that humans are totally material; others claiming that the body is merely an inhibiting shell for the "real" person existing within it). Karl Rahner stressed the necessity of appreciating the integral unity of body and soul as the basis for receiving Christian mysteries. He said that the realities of Christian faith

> can only be presented adequately when the bodily reality of man, and so his acts in the dimensions of space and time, history and society, are conceived of as symbolic realities embodying his person and its primordial decisions. This would be the real starting-point for reaching an understanding of the historically attainable life of the Church as symbolic embodiment of the Spirit of God and of the inner history of the dialogue between God's free love and human freedom.[36]

What does Rahner mean by saying that the bodily reality of human life and human actions must be understood as "symbolic realities"? In his brilliant essay on "The Theology of Symbol" he pointed beyond the ordinary ways in which the term "symbol" is used, to a deeper meaning that "is much more obscure, difficult and ambiguous than is usually thought."[37] By "real symbol" he meant that every being is symbolic *in itself* before it merely refers to something else. Right within its own existence, every being *expresses* itself–and this expression *is* its symbolic reality. This is the primordial meaning of symbol and it is "initially present in the depths of the grounds of each one's being."[38] All derivative meanings of the term "symbol" flow from this. For human persons, *the body is each one's "real symbol."* Every woman, man and child is a mysterious union of soul and body, matter and spirit, but the human body is the "real symbol" which makes the person known in the world.

Symbolic reality in all created beings reflects trinitarian life. Rahner saw such significance in the understanding of symbolic reality that he regarded all theology to be incomprehensible if it would not be a theology of symbols. The starting point for such a theological unfolding, he said, is found in Jesus Christ, and more particularly in his saying, "To have seen me is to have seen the Father" (Jn 14:9). Regarding the incarnation, Rahner said:

> [T]he incarnate word is the absolute symbol of God in the world, filled as nothing else can be with what is symbolized. He is not merely the presence and revelation of what God is in himself. He is also the expressive presence of what–or rather, who–God wished to be, in free grace, to the world, in such a way that this divine attitude, once so expressed, can never be reversed, but is and remains final and unsurpassable.[39]

It is this level of symbolic reality that is crucial for a theological understanding of mutuality. From the moment of conception through the moment of death, *the human body is a person's real symbol.* Unless that is understood, the outward expression of mutuality can be interpreted superficially. When symbolic reality is understood, there is a realization that *the outward expression is at once the very person* expressed in the world, the person totally implicated in whatever is lived out through the body. In matters of mutuality this cannot be overstressed since mutuality can be lived only in and through the body, which is the outward symbolic reality of the whole person.

Rahner showed how the doctrines of faith interpenetrate one another and how crucial it is to appreciate the body as real symbol in order to receive the mysteries of Christian faith. The body expresses the whole person, makes the entire person known. The soul is not a vapor residing in a limited portion of the body (such as the brain). It is pervasive of the entire lived body. This ontological wholeness of the person gives immense dignity to every distinguishable power or "part." Or, in Rahner's words: "This symbolic relationship of the part of the body to the original whole, from which the part derives, may vary in intensity in different parts of the body, but it can never be entirely absent wherever a given part is substantially informed by the soul."[40]

As symbolic reality, the body is an outward expression of the whole person's values, intentions, emotions, thoughts and choices. Before anyone chooses to reveal self verbally, there is a bodily manifestation of self. It is this living body, this seemingly incongruous union of matter and spirit, that is called to be the image of God, called to be person-gift, without division or dissimulation.

For this call to be perfectly realized there would have to be a complete integrity in this union–the outward symbolic reality truly expressing the total person. To put it more informally: there would need to be perfect harmony between the "within" and the "without." In wounded humanity, this integrity can only be partial, except for Jesus Christ and his redeemed Mother. St. Paul, for example, expressed his anguish over the self-division he knew: "I cannot understand my own behaviour. I fail to carry out the things I want to do, and I find myself doing the very things I hate" (Rom 7:15).

Integrity is the core of both symbolic reality and genuine mutuality. The more integrally the body expresses the whole person, the more it is a "real symbol," open to realizing the call to be image of trinitarian love. On the other hand, the greater the variance between a person's thoughts, emotions and choices–and their outward bodily expression–the more diminished is self-realization and the earthly imaging of God.

This is evident in sexual intercourse. Despite the recent flurry of books (secular, theological and pastoral) and videos dealing with human sexuality, only a few give evidence of recognizing the immense significance of its meaning and the call for integrity in every sexual act which expresses and implicates the whole person. There is what I term a "macro and micro" potential for union in every marital act of genital intercourse. First, there is the "macro" union: the person-gift between spouses, body to body. When this remains unblocked, open to the transmission of life, there is simultaneously the potential for a "micro" union between ovum and sperm: a mutual indwelling that is the new, forever life of the child.

While the "macro" union is brief, temporary, and recedes into physical separateness again, the micro union which may result from uninhibited self-gift is permanent, inextricable, and personal. Even a *minimal* understanding of this exchange makes it evident why each act of spousal intercourse is to remain open to the transmission of life in ways that are responsible and integral. The dignity of marital intimacy and the need for personal presence and mutual assent in each act is also evident once there is even an elemental understanding of the body as "real symbol." The body is our primary location of personal presence, says Arthur Vogel. It enables us to *be* our words, "or, as it is usually put, mean what we say."[41] Word and speaker comprise a unity, whether the "word" is verbal or is expressed in body-language. People are asked to "stand behind" their words. Deceit, says Vogel, is trying to "stand in two places at the same time":

> It is man's nature to be body-meaning and a word; he has no choice about the matter. He does have a choice, however, about what he says as a body-word.... Christians see Jesus Christ as the fulfillment of man as a body-word, a fulfillment so complete that it amounts to man's recreation.[42]

Vogel is using sacramental language here. Jesus Christ is the perfect fulfillment of the human potential to be body-word, given in self-gift and longing for a mutual response. *How dazzlingly improbable that the union of matter and human spirit can be the image of God, forever living in self-gift.* Perhaps no one in this century has probed this more deeply than Pope John Paul II in his several-year series of audiences on body theology and marriage. Commenting on Adam's cry of recognition upon beholding Eve ("This is bone of my bones and flesh of my flesh"), John Paul said: "Exclaiming in this way, he seems to say: here is *a body that expresses the 'person'!*"[43] It was a recognition of sinless symbolic reality. It also was a crying out for the imaging of divine mutual love. Since the function of an image is to reflect the model, woman and man become the image of God not so much in their moments of solitude as in their moments of communion. Human beings are called to be the image of "an inscrutable divine communion of Persons."[44]

Humanity Emerges in the Dimension of Mutual Gift

This personal communion in God is perichoretic; it is a life of indwelling and reciprocal self-gift. To be created in that image means that humanity emerges in history in the dimension of mutual gift, which can only be lived out bodily. In one of his 1980 papal audiences, John Paul II said that he wanted to introduce "a new dimension, a new criterion of understanding and interpretation, which we will call 'hermeneutics of the gift'" since the dimension of gift is "at the heart of the mystery of creation."[45]

John Paul designates gift as the fundamental characteristic of human existence. To be human is to be created as person-gift, to be given and received in relationship. That is why John Paul describes the body's basic meaning as "nuptial," a meaning knowable both through revelation and human discovery. This is no sentimental metaphor–the nuptial meaning of body "is the fundamental element of human existence in the world."[46] Now, it is nearly identical to say 1) that gift is the fundamental characteristic of human existence, and 2) that the nuptial meaning of body is the fundamental element of human existence in the world. To be created in God's image is to be created for "nuptial" expression.

At first it may seem startling, even too limiting, to designate body-meaning as nuptial, since *meaning* is at the depths of ontological significance and in this case applies universally to every human body. The nuptial significance of body is not restricted to marriage; it names the meaning of body at every stage of development and in every state of life. At the basic level of body meaning there is the call to be image of God's unitive life. It means a bodily giving and receiving that is lived out in ways that are appropriate to each "You" encountered in relationship. It is the vocation to be a living gift. John Paul says that both married and celibate love are to be "conjugal," that is, bearing the total gift of oneself. Each in its unique way expresses that conjugal body meaning that is inscribed in woman and man, in what it means to be a human person. Whatever the specific vocation of a human person, there is need to develop an adequate language of the body to express its profound nuptial meaning, in fidelity. This requires mutual integrity, so that the actions of the body fulfill in truth what is appropriate in each encounter.

Gift and the Nuptial Meaning of Body

Within a *Donum* theology or theology of gift, the body is perceived as nuptial and gift is considered the basic category of being. It is in this light that human mutuality becomes clearer, enabling one to see that 1) mutuality involves the total person; 2) mutuality requires integrity; and 3) mutuality as person-gift is intrinsically risky, making a person vulnerable. It has been shown how trinitarian mutuality means complete reciprocity of person-gift. In human relationships, person-gift involves the "nuptial body," appropriately given and received, and there is no substitute for total self-gift. Derivatively, all giving of gifts (even at great personal cost) has meaning only to the extent that the gifts are honest extensions of the self-gift they signify. Jesus underscored this when he observed the widow placing two coins into the temple collection. He praised her because she gave not of her abundance but of her life sustenance.

Troubling questions arise from saying that mutuality involves the total person. How is this possible when there are such varying levels of relationship? Further, how is it possible to live mutual self-gift in a wounded humanity without being devastated or severely misunderstood? These are serious questions.

The first question is particularly troubling within western culture for two reasons: a) it is often assumed that total bodily self-gift must be expressed in some genital fashion, radically curtailing the nuptial meaning of body; and b) through a variety of technical means, it is possible to partition and manipulate aspects of embodied gift, even while "going through the motions" of seeming to be giving one's self. In both instances the human potential for mutuality is severely diminished. It is now possible in western societies to separate unitive and procreative aspects of the conjugal act; to separate the conception of a child from intercourse; and to separate gametes from parental bodies for various delayed combinations under laboratory conditions. This diminishes or bypasses the expression of "real symbol." Reciprocal gift, then, is frequently replaced by isolated choices, convenience, or commercial transactions. Robert Brungs asks:

> Is the human body a proper object of scientific and technological manipulation, using "manipulation" in a completely neutral sense? More specifically, is there something in our bodies, or something about them–in their shape, texture and function–that should not be altered, that is in some sense consecrated?
>
> Such questions cannot at this time be answered with any doctrinal sureness or confidence. In the face of.... momentous advances in the life sciences (and in other areas of Christian living as well) it is absolutely necessary to engage in the significant development of our doctrine on the meaning of our bodiedness. We do not have the luxury of a leisurely approach to this issue.[47]

Concerns about bodily nuptiality go beyond questions of manipulation, however. There are so many levels of relationship. How can any person honestly live mutual self-gift in and through the body among the multiple relationships that span an ordinary life? The gospels are instructive here. In spare, straightforward accounts the writers show how Jesus consistently discerned the most appropriate manner of expressing his self-gift, whatever the circumstance. In spite of this he *was* misunderstood and maligned. The Bread of Life Discourse (Jn 6) provides a consummate example of his followers' inability to receive his promise of self-gift as food and drink. Although they had been miraculously fed and had pursued him for further favors, they recoiled at his offer of complete, embodied self-gift. Jesus did not retract the offer. The very possibility of mutual response meant respecting their freedom. It was essential, however, that he maintain the possibility of response to his offer of total self-gift. Only a few would remain after he revealed:

> [M]y flesh is real food
> and my blood is real drink.
> He who eats my flesh and drinks my blood
> lives in me
> and I live in him (Jn 6:55–56).

The current climate of thought in the west makes it difficult for many

Christians to affirm that mutual self-gift involves the total body-person.

While the second mark of mutuality–integrity–is closely allied to the first (total personal involvement), it requires specific emphasis. Despite the radical difference between divine and human self-gift, and despite the woundedness and weakness of human love, every man, woman and child is invited to share in perichoretic life. Jesus' prayer at the last supper indicated that mutual indwelling love did not depend upon identity of natures, but upon integral response to divine self-gift. The third eucharistic prayer asks that those nourished by Christ's body and blood "may be filled with his Holy Spirit, and become one body, one spirit in Christ." Then, significantly, the prayer asks that the Holy Spirit "make us an everlasting gift to you." The relation between the Father and the worshiping community is expressed in terms of gift, the community identifying with the self-gift of the Son, in the Holy Spirit. The need for integrity is evident. While this may be transparent in liturgical and doctrinal spheres, it is less clear in daily life.

For that reason, it is imperative to search for living examples of those who affirm the need to strive for this integrity, to pray for its realization in their lives. As will be seen in the following chapters, it was the longing for this integrity that fired Father Raymond Ellis and the people of St. Cecilia Parish in Detroit to be concerned about art and plumbing and garbage as a way of preparing integrally for their eucharistic offering of gifts. And it was this need for integrity that stirred teenagers in Rome to work with disadvantaged immigrants if they were to receive the gospels authentically. It was this drive for integrity in their married love that moved couples in the eastern United States to form a community that would enable their growing fidelity in self-gift.

Living the gift of one's body is an awesome task and there is a constant tension in maintaining personal unity in a sin-wounded world. Philosopher Richard Zaner describes a kind of "chill" that accompanies growing awareness of the way in which the total person is implicated in every human act. "As little Emily in Richard Hughes' novel, *A High Wind in Jamaica*.... says, experiencing her own embodiment, 'You can't get out of it now, not for a long time!'"[48] Zaner writes of the human person as a complexity of intimacy and aloneness, of functions, members, systems and performances that form a single event, or what he has called "a living *integrity*." Embodied life involves effort, tasks, and self-sacrifice if integral growth is to happen.

In a society rife with division and deception it may seem incongruous for Christians to affirm that a growing integrity is possible through graced relationships with divine persons–this in spite of all temptations to misuse the gift of the body. In one of his audiences Pope John Paul II considered the question: do Christ's words have enduring validity, or has contemporary humanity outgrown them? In response to this question which is voiced with some frequency now, the pope stressed that there is an essential truth about humanity itself found in Christ's words, a truth that has enduring validity. Christ did not artificially ask that human hearts return to a pre-Fall innocence (a condition forever left behind after original sin). Rather, he pointed to a purity of heart that is both possible and accessible even in a condition of hereditary sinfulness. John Paul described this as "the purity of the man of lust who is entirely enveloped by the 'redemption of the body' carried out by Christ."[49] There is a wonderful incongruity here which can evoke joyful laughter for those seeking integrity: "the purity of the man of lust" can be affirmed because nothing is impossible to God.

The third characteristic of human mutuality, understood within a theology of gift, is this: it is marked by risk and vulnerability. In divine mutuality, there is free, abiding donation of self-gift, without domination or self-seeking. Among us, created free in a sin-laced world, self-gift can result in betrayal and harm. The nuptial meaning of body must be upheld in the midst of abrasive contacts, divisions, deceptions, lust, and domination. Abruptly put, it is the purity of the redeemed lustful person. "Lust" is not restricted to the sexual/genital sphere. It refers to every form of human "taking" rather than giving and receiving. Likewise, purity of heart refers to a guileless honesty that is pervasive of the entire person. Jesus counseled his followers to be wise as serpents and simple as doves, knowing the risks they would have to undertake in witnessing bodily to all that had been entrusted to them. Jesus became vulnerable to vicious, degrading attacks upon his person and ultimately endured a humiliating death because his self-gift was rejected. Rather than negating the possibility of that gift, Christ's vulnerability unto death made it the very possibility of his timeless self-gift in the risen body and the blood. The reconciliation of these seeming contradictories opened the possibility of divine-human mutual gift through every human generation.

Bringing Life's Incongruities to New Synthesis

In my university classes dealing with a Christian understanding of body and matter, I ask students to reflect upon their positive and negative experiences of embodiment. One young man wrote of near-despair following the termination of a dishonest sexual relationship:

> A part that was truly scary in my life at this point was that I did not feel fully human. I had little, if any self-esteem. I remember one time before getting into the shower, standing at the mirror looking at my body, I felt nauseated. I could not stand to see myself and I had wished so much to be rid of my body.[50]

At that moment, seeing an image of his divided self nauseated him, making it impossible for him to receive his embodiment as gift. Sometimes such awareness proves the breakthrough moment, initiating the desire for integrity. The pain that comes from recognizing the disparities and limitations, the awful risks in self-giving can become a form of prayer. Augustine cried out, "You have made us toward yourself and our hearts are restless until they rest in you." Citing the crucial distinctions between divine and human love, Rémi Brague notes:

> In a word, human love is limited (which allows it to be sinful, that is to change to its opposite) because what joins us to the beloved does not exhaust what we are. The relation which joins us to another is not the same thing as our nature. In other words, love is something we feel, something we experience, something we possess, or however we want to put it–but it is never by itself what we *are*. [51]

Nevertheless, nuptial *meaning* inheres in the human body, together with a longing for perfect union. There is a restless desire to penetrate and be penetrated not only by divine and human persons, but the universe itself. Sometimes this is voiced as the desire to experience the unknown, in ways that transcend any previous encounter. People walk ever deeper into forests, slip into dark crevices of the earth, process into shrines and arenas. The warrior-Caesars of the Roman Empire constructed memorial arches through which they might enter a land and people. The human longing to penetrate and be penetrated is lived out on a continuum from loving self-giving and receiving to lustful domination. The unslaked desire for commingling endures.

I recall this yearning in a young man who operated a funicular on a halcyon October day in Grindelwald, Switzerland. Hang gliders in multicolored splendor drifted into the glacial valley from surrounding mountaintops. While his hand regulated the turnstile his body leaned toward those who were riding the air currents. When I asked if he were a glider he responded like one who saw the heavens opened before him, saying it was the best thing he had ever done. He lived a paradox: while operating the funicular, its closed capsules filled with passengers moving up and down the mountainside in perfect equilibrium and predictability, he longed for the near-mystical act of pushing off a mountaintop, penetrating and being penetrated by the color-spangled valley.

There is a similarity between the operator's brief, intense words and the reflections of a university student who sky dives but also is attuned to his environment:

> I don't pretend to know God in a physical way, but I do know him in a real way. It's almost like walking into a house and being overwhelmed by the smell of freshly-baked bread. In a very real way you "know" the bread even though you can't see the loaf. Sometimes I like to think of my spiritual growth as a sharpening of my sense of smell.

Of sky-diving, he described the sensory overload, the rush of adrenaline that accompanied his first free-fall. His second jump was different:

> This time it was almost a religious experience. It was like standing on top of a mountain, only there was no mountain. I thanked God, while in the air, for allowing me to experience the medium of our environment as so few have the opportunity to do. I marvelled at the world while suspended in a jelloed atmosphere–the experience moved me like no other.

The transcendence experienced in human/nonhuman relations derives ultimately from inner divine life. The exhilaration of hang gliding and skydiving comes from a commingling with the earth that is untrammeled by compulsion or domination. In each case there must be a respect for air, wind and gravity, as well as respect for bodily limitations and the fragile combinations of cloth and cord laced across an open sky. In "free-fall," freedom means moving together with the elements of earth. Defying even one of them means death. It is a parable for the mutual relations between women and men, between races, cultures and nations. Pope John Paul II, speaking of the man-woman relation, reflects: "'From the beginning' the woman is entrusted to his [man's] eyes, to his consciousness, to his sensitivity, to his 'heart'. He, on the other hand, must, in a way, ensure the same process of the exchange of the gift, the mutual interpenetration of giving and receiving as a gift, which, precisely through its reciprocity, creates a real communion of persons."[52]

There is enormous tension between the call to be person-gift and the risk of being used or dominated. Christian spirituality consistently emphasizes self-gift in divine and human love, while late twentieth century mass media emphasize in stark imagery the reality of abuse and degradations of persons. The latter tend to arouse fear of self-gift, interpreting it frequently as subservience or a patriarchal imposition. There is no risk-free mutuality. It is marked by the cross and reconciled only in the fullness of the paschal mystery.

CHAPTER FOUR

The Church as Sacrament of Trinitarian Mutuality

> From the communion that Christians experience in Christ there immediately flows the communion which they experience with one another: all are branches of a single vine, namely, Christ. In this communion is the wonderful reflection and participation in the mystery of the intimate life of love in God as Trinity, Father, Son and Holy Spirit as revealed by the Lord Jesus.... *Such communion is the very mystery of the Church,* as the Second Vatican Council recalls in the celebrated words of St. Cyprian: "The Church shines forth as 'a people made one with the unity of the Father, Son and Holy Spirit.' "
>
> –*Vocation and Mission of the Lay Faithful* [1]

The church is called to be a sacrament of trinitarian communion, outwardly manifesting the effective presence of God in the world. But two questions persist regarding this mystery: 1) *Concretely,* how does the church sacramentalize the mutual self-giving and receiving of divine persons? and 2) Why is the eucharist the basis and center for building the faith community precisely as an image of divine mutual self-gift? Throughout this reflection on mutuality we are grappling not only with its *meaning,* but the *possibility* of its realization in human relations with God, other people, and the nonpersonal universe. Thus, these practical questions are vital in deepening a spirituality of interpersonal relations. If mutuality were simply an abstract ideal without any evidence of its realization in homes, parishes, and the marketplace, it would be a cruel mirage deceiving those who pursue it.

Far from being an elusive mirage, mutuality is constitutive of the church as a mystery of communion, and I suggest that it is tangible in specific faith communities. Prior to looking at these specific examples in parishes and local communities, however, we should be able to find trinitarian patterns in the universal church–patterns that transcend cultures, languages and economic conditions.

Since the Second Vatican Council there has been a restlessness (more accurately, a nagging anxiety) within the Roman Catholic Church regarding the unique identities and relationships among the laity, clergy and religious. This restlessness and struggle for clarification indicate a paradigm shift in the inner life of the church, at the very time that there is an awakening to its trinitarian dimensions. It is an apt moment for speculation on the immense potential of these interrelationships. While there are numerous "trinities within trinities" within the church, I would like to propose one possible pattern within the Roman Catholic communion. It is this: within the one people of God, the laity sacramentalize in a particular manner the giving and receiving of God the Father; those in the ordained priesthood uniquely sacramentalize the Son's giving and receiving; and those in consecrated religious life sacramentalize the person of the Holy Spirit. All of this is said by way of analogy. Just as in appropriating specific characteristics to any person of the Trinity, it must be kept in mind that what is appropriated to one is somehow common to all. So, too, in appropriating a predominant manner of imaging trinitarian love to laity, clergy or religious, we must be mindful that all share in the full triune life.

The Laity: Image of the First Person

Although the analogy proposed here may be unfamiliar, there is a certain fittingness in attributing the human imaging of God the Father to the laity. In the Old Testament, God was revealed primarily through activities and characteristics which Christians later appropriated to the first person of the Trinity, the one whom Jesus called his Father. It is useful to consider some of these attributes in order to see why the laity image them in a unique manner.

In Genesis the loving, prolific creator establishes a balance between order and freedom, and initiates a universe refulgent with interrelated possibilities. Dynamic generativity and tender nurturing characterize this personal God who holds all life into diverse becoming. Phyllis Trible shows how the Old Testament writers employed the Hebrew word for womb, *rehem,* to describe the compassionate, maternal divine care.[2] For Sarah, Leah and Hannah, control of the womb "belongs neither to women nor to their husbands, neither to the fetus nor to society. Only God closes and opens wombs in judgment, in blessing, and in mystery."[3] But more is implied than God's activities in creation. There is a quality *in* God that is likened to enwombing. Commenting on God's tender relations with the house of Jacob, Trible says:

> God conceives in the womb; God fashions in the womb; God judges in the womb; God destines in the womb; God brings forth from the womb; God receives out of the womb; and God carries from the womb to gray hairs. From this uterine perspective, then, Yahweh molds life for individuals and for the nation Israel. Accordingly, in biblical traditions an organ unique to the female becomes a vehicle pointing to the compassion of God.[4]

The Hebrew noun *rah^{a}mîm* (plural of *rehem,* womb) denotes the virtues of mercy, compassion and love. It is significant, then, that Pope John Paul II began his encyclical letter *On the Mercy of God* in this fashion: "It is 'God, who is rich in mercy' (Eph 2:4) whom Jesus has revealed to us as Father."[5] The entire encyclical hinges on the Father's mercy and its meaning for the mission of the church: women and men of faith will attain to God's merciful love to the extent that their interior lives are transformed through unifying mutual love. Where this is genuinely present it will be manifest in their life-style. Merciful love is never a unilateral act. Although it may seem that in some interchanges only one person does the giving while the other merely receives (e.g., physicians in their care of the sick; teachers in conducting classes; parents in raising their children; benefactors in helping the needy), in reality the one who gives also receives. This is crucial in mutual love: the one who extends merciful love also is a beneficiary of it.[6]

John Paul dwells on this mutual quality of merciful love, citing Christ crucified as the loftiest "disquieting model" of it: the one who opened divine mercy to all who would receive it also accepted any mercy extended to others as shown personally to him. "An act of merciful love is only really such when we are deeply convinced at the moment that we perform it that we are at the same time receiving mercy from the people who are accepting it from us."[7] This reciprocity indicates that the most perfect incarnation of *equality* among people is to be found in genuine Christian mercy. It is simultaneously the most perfect incarnation of justice. Today there is a universal cry for justice, but of itself justice cannot establish mutual bonds. When tender mercy is wedded to justice, however, there is reverence for the dignity of each person, and this enables a genuine mutual exchange.

In Jesus' teaching there was a specific revelation of the *Father* as creator and nurturer. Through the parables of the prodigal son, the lost sheep and the lost coin, he showed that the merciful love of God is marked by cordial tenderness and sensitivity. Since merciful love is essential for mutual relationships (justice never sufficing in itself) it is supremely indispensable for those in closest relationship: husbands and wives, parents and children, friends, and those in pastoral service.[8] Jesus does not limit the Father's characteristics to creativity and merciful love, however. In a variety of parables the Father is likened to a prudent king, to the owner of a vineyard, to a grieving parent who awaits the return of a wayward child. The Father "works" and creates persons in the divine image who will share responsibility for the care of the earth.

It seems apparent that the *laity*, women and men together, image in a particular manner the first person of the Trinity–creator, prolific merciful lover, sustainer of the universe, totally given in self-gift to the Son and the Holy Spirit. In their mission within the church, the laity bear distinct responsibility for creative stewardship of the earth, and through their fertile, mutual love they share this mission in continuity with daughters and sons. To the laity is entrusted in a particular manner responsibility for the development of the temporal order–from responsible gene splicing, to honest political campaigns and a caring distribution of the world's wheat and oil.

The gospel parables depict the Father's concern for the human family. In "tending the vineyard," the Father is not only concerned for the unemployed who stand in the marketplace, but also for those whose work conditions harm them and those who are denied the development of their talents. In the parables, Jesus gives the first person the role of a competent administrator, one who seeks co-laborers and invites their personal initiative, one who takes business trips and longs for honest accountability. There is no condescension in the divine administrator's expectations of women and men: all are called to their fullest potential.

Today those who image the Father must be astute in conserving the gifts of the earth, and wise in their promotion of life-enhancing technologies. It is urgent that persons of faith, rich in mercy and capable of mutual self-gift assume these responsibilities. The laity's imaging of the Father seems evident in the recent apostolic exhortation on the *Vocation and Mission of the Lay Faithful:*

> In order to achieve their task directed to the Christian animation of the temporal order, in the sense of serving persons and society, the lay faithful *are never to relinquish their participation in "public life,"* that is, in the many different economic, social, legislative, administrative and cultural areas, which are intended to promote organically and institutionally the *common good.*[9]

"In the Person of Christ"

While it may at first be uncomfortable to think of the laity as imaging the first person of the Trinity in a special manner, it is familiar to think and speak about the ordained clergy in the likeness of the second person, the Son or Word. In the church's recent attempts to delineate with greater clarity the meaning of sacramental ordination, there is frequent reference to the ordained priest as being *in persona Christi* (in the person of Christ). If this is to be appreciated as more than an honorary designation, it is necessary to see why those anointed as priests are said to be "in the person of Christ" in a unique manner, and what principal activities and attributes appropriated to the second person of the Trinity relate in a special way to them. Once again, it is clear that human imaging of the Word is not an exclusive prerogative of the clergy. The *Pastoral Constitution on the Church in the Modern World* makes this clear, noting that in some fashion, Christ united himself with every human person, working with his hands, thinking with a human mind and acting by human choice. To be *in persona Christi* is a specific calling, but it does not exclude the rest of the church body from witnessing the presence of Christ in a sacramental world.

What activities and qualities of the second person, then, are particularly imaged by priests? Both the *mission* of the eternal Word within human history and his *self-characterization,* as reported in the gospels, provide the basis for understanding how priests are marked in the image of the Son of God made man. In a manner that is distinct from the Father and the Holy Spirit, the Son accomplished a redemptive mission in the flesh. He was sent on this mission from within the triune communion of persons. The letter to the Hebrews speaks of Christ's earthly mission in terms of priesthood–showing how he differed in this regard from the high priests of the Hebrew covenant. The letter details how high priests were taken from the Jewish community and appointed to act on the people's behalf in relation to God, especially through offering gifts and sacrifices. None "took" this priesthood of his own accord; each was called by God. Likewise, Christ did not appoint himself as priest of the new covenant, "but he had it from the one who said to him: *You are my son, today I have become your father*" (Heb 5:5). Jesus Christ's mission is that of personal self-gift, and all Christian priesthood is centered in that same mission. Jesus became the living enfleshment of divine mutual self-giving. He assumed into his person the division, violence, and selfishness of all humanity–not to condemn, but to redeem through total self-sacrifice in perpetuity. All Christian sacrifice *is* self-gift. Sent on mission and anointed by the "Spirit of the Lord" (see Lk 4:18) Christ gave himself for the salvation of all who would receive that gift.

As with all mysteries of faith, the Christ-identity requires a number of images and analogies to make it more accessible to human understanding and response. In unfolding his identity to the first disciples, Jesus described himself as bridegroom, shepherd, servant, bread of life, and "the way, the truth and the life." Each of these self-identifying images indicates that Jesus chose to be self-gift, to be the available one poured out for others.

Although every member of the church is to manifest characteristics of the incarnate Son of God, those anointed and consecrated as priests are to bear his image in a manner that marks their very existence. When it is said that priests act *in persona Christi* it is important to recall what was said earlier in this work about the meaning of symbolic reality and the need for integrity in the outward expression of personal unity. It is the entire person that is marked or "characterized" in the sacrament of holy orders. Priesthood is not simply a matter of function: it is a personal identity which can be named *in persona Christi.* The ministerial priesthood and the priesthood of the baptized are "ordered to one another," yet they remain distinct not only in degree but also in essence.[10] This distinction is significant for our discussion of the church's imaging of divine mutual love.

In his 1989 Holy Thursday Letter to Priests, Pope John Paul II reminded them how Christ was appointed to act on behalf of the whole people, and how each priest is to act on behalf of the whole community in relation to God, especially in the eucharist. In his encyclical *Redemptor Hominis* he placed this within the context of self-gift: "In Christ, priesthood is linked with His sacrifice, His self-giving to the Father; and precisely because it is without limit, that self-giving gives rise in us human beings subject to numerous limitations the need to turn to God in an ever more mature way and with a constant, ever more profound, conversion."[11]

Within the Roman Catholic rite, service "in the person of Christ" is perceived within a profound sacramental understanding of body. Priestly celibacy expresses Christ's identity as bridegroom of the church. In authentic celibate love, a priest's body is nuptial in the manner of Christ–not in covenant with one woman, expressed genitally, but in committed nuptial love for the body of Christ, expressed appropriately, bodily, in total self-gift to the community served. Whether he presides at eucharist or sacramentalizes the forgiving presence of Christ in the sacrament of reconciliation, a priest images the risen Christ, living and effectively present in the community. Like the good shepherd who is prepared to give his life for those entrusted to his leadership, a priest who acts in the person of Christ does more than perform functions; his being is marked for enduring self-gift. When a priest actually lives his service to a people in this fashion, it can be startlingly effective, as will be seen in the example of Father Raymond Ellis, whose pastorate in inner city Detroit will be discussed in the following chapter.

In beginning his public ministry, Jesus identified with the anointed servant of Isaiah 61:1–2. He had been sent to bring good news to the poor, to set captives free, give sight to the blind, liberate the downtrodden, and proclaim the "Lord's year of favor." On the threshold of his public ministry Jesus made it clear that *he personified the text which he had been invited to proclaim.* That is also the vocation of priests ordained to serve "in his person." In that sense the collegial body of ordained priests forms a hierarchy of service. Commenting on this term which was employed by the Second Vatican Council, John Paul reminded fellow priests that "It is 'hierarchical' in the sense of sacred service. For 'hierarchy' means sacred governance, which in the church is service."[12] In Christ, service is never simply a philanthropic donation or a temporary function: it is committed self-giving for the benefit of all.

All this is brought to mind here in reference to mutuality, that interflow of giving and receiving which is reciprocal, not one-dimensional or isolated. Both lay and ordained forms of priesthood express in complementary ways the *one* priesthood of Christ. But this does not yet express the full trinitarian pattern. *Within* the common priesthood of the baptized there is a "third" dimension of the church, formed by women and men vowed in religious life. It must now be seen how the imaging of the Holy Spirit can be appropriated to them in a particular manner.

Religious and the "Second Counsellor"

Full dogmatic clarity regarding the trinitarian identity of the Holy Spirit came only in the fourth century although the third person's dynamic indwelling of the church was experienced from its inception. It is interesting that the fourth century also witnessed the "move to the desert" and the beginnings of "religious" life.

Just as it was necessary to sketch the characteristics of the Father and the Son to see how laity and clergy aptly image them, so it is important to consider what qualities are attributed to the Holy Spirit in order to see if, analogously, women and men religious bear a particular likeness to the third person. It is difficult to select major qualities of the Spirit because of the fertile richness of concrete images used to describe this person! In the Old Testament, God's Spirit (*ruach* = wind, breath) is recognized through three predominant emphases: 1) God's awesome power; 2) the divine source of inspiration (sometimes a kind of possession, accompanied by ecstatic phenomena); and 3) the divine presence within the covenanted community.[13]

The New Testament describes the Holy Spirit more diversely

and personally than the Old Testament does. In his farewell discourse alone, Jesus names the Spirit whom he and the Father will send: the Advocate (counsellor), teacher, witness and Spirit of truth. In the Acts of the Apostles the Holy Spirit is designated "personal gift" (2:38) and the source of gifts within the community (10:45). St. Paul celebrates the variety and abundance of the Spirit's gifts, but assures the early church that all of these gifts derive from the one Spirit. From its origins the church acknowledged the Holy Spirit as the supreme enabler who makes the ongoing mission of Christ effective among the people of God. St. Paul, for example, noted that no one is able to say "Jesus is Lord" apart from the influence of the Holy Spirit. It is the Holy Spirit who anoints for specific tasks, confirms the hesitant and prods the reluctant. Employing a rush of words, reminiscent of Pentecostal winds, Karl Rahner and Herbert Vorgrimler describe the third person in this manner:

> Because God creates as God, he creates as Spirit everything in the world that is constantly new and fresh, free and vital, unexpected and mighty, at once tender and strong: the mystery of love, which even in the natural world is always the most intimate mystery. He is the Spirit of grace: God within us as our anointing and sealing, our earnest of heaven, our guest, comforter and advocate, the interior call, freedom and sonship, life and peace, holiness and unity, we call the Spirit.[14]

The Holy Spirit's presence is unpredictable by human calculations. The unlikely complex of images used to sign the Spirit indicate this: tongues of fire, gale-force winds, intimate breath and a tranquil dove. Of the three divine persons, it is the Holy Spirit who most pointedly exemplifies the *incongruous* quality of mystery which has been discussed earlier. Designated as the faithful, enduring indweller of the church and every Christian, the Holy Spirit nevertheless comes and goes with the swiftness and subtlety of wind, falling upon believers as personal fire and enabling the "impossible." At times the Spirit sends messengers ahead (the annunciation being the most eloquent example); at other times the Spirit intervenes directly, as Peter learned early in his ministry.[15] What became increasingly clear during the first centuries of Christian experience was the Holy Spirit's unique identity as the love of the Trinity in person, the personal bond of Father and Son.

Jesus, himself anointed and led by the Spirit, invited his followers to know a holy freedom in allowing the Holy Spirit's loving, effective interchange with them. He counseled lack of anxiety and a nonclutching attitude toward other persons and the good things of earth. Sometimes Jesus' evaluations of reality startled his contemporaries since they cut across conventional wisdom: the heart is the ultimate receptacle of treasure; bulging barns and seats at the head table can thus be exceeded by two coins in the alms box; the highest form of love is self-gift unto death. Upon Jesus' invitation, Peter, James and John left parents, boat and fishing nets immediately to follow him (the rich young man who received a similar invitation declined it). Yet, Jesus counseled them to wait upon their post-resurrection mission until they had received the gift of the Holy Spirit. Only then would they fling open the doors of the upper room where they had been fearfully gathered. Only then could they proclaim the paschal mystery joyfully and openly, relying on the effective, miraculous presence of Christ among them.

Christians kept this Spirit-filled vibrancy during the intermittent persecutions of the first three centuries and the "hidden" days of the early church. With the "Constantinian turn" of the fourth century, however, many people found that it was economically and politically advantageous to be identified as Christian. In order to maintain the integrity of their faith, people such as Antony of Egypt and Pachomius took up residence in the desert, where they might pray and know the freedom of heart which Jesus had counseled. These men and women of the desert provided the beginning structures of vowed religious life–a way of living gospel poverty, consecrated celibacy, and Spirit-centered obedience.

Being an image of the gift of the Holy Spirit for the benefit of the entire people of God requires a holy freedom from all that would hinder a Spirit-impelled life. When understood and lived authentically, the vows professed by religious assure a growth in such freedom. They are not taken out of disdain for the good things of creation, but precisely to affirm a nonpossessive appreciation for them. It would be difficult to find any vowed religious who expressed this loving reception of all creation as gift more than St. Francis of Assisi. Like the Holy Spirit, those freed by choice from personal *ownership* of material things can simultaneously 1) be personally present to the community and 2) come and go responsibly at the Spirit's bidding. The vow of obedience is intended as a means of freeing religious for the ways of the Spirit. Through dialogue and prayerful discernment, the individual religious and the whole community are open to the guidance of the unpredictable, loving Spirit. By the vow of celibacy, *a woman or man promises to be embodied self-gift,* imaging in a particular manner the Holy Spirit as personal love and bond. While bodily affirming the supreme value of divine love, a vowed religious takes on the responsibility of indwelling the community as personal love, as a bonding point between clergy and laity.

Religious communities are deliberately identified and named within the church when they clearly express a charism of the Holy Spirit for the benefit of all. The rich variety of communities is indicative of the Spirit's vital, ongoing activity. Writing shortly after the Second Vatican Council, Pope Paul VI said that the gospel witness of religious life manifests the primacy of God's love "with a force for which We must give thanks to the Holy Spirit."[16] Far from being simply a human impulse or one derived from a mentality conformed to the modern world, religious life "is the fruit of the Holy Spirit, who is always at work within the Church."[17]

From this brief consideration of one trinitarian pattern in the church, it seems evident that laity, clergy and vowed religious, together forming one communion in Christ, nevertheless can image unique aspects of trinitarian self-gift with singular clarity. This puts flesh on assertions about perichoretic love that might otherwise remain very abstract. George Maloney stresses that the "trinitarian reality is to be experienced now. The doctrine of the Trinity is not only what makes Christians uniquely different from all other religions, but it is a reality that effects the fulfillment of our very being as human persons."[18] Once members of the church recognize how the trinitarian reality can characterize their daily encounters, they will begin to see that *this is the design of all Christian life and relationship*. Where this is *lived,* even in a stumbling fashion, the unique gifts of each are recognized and appreciated (without any one member of the three-in-one-body struggling to dominate and without an insistence on sameness of ministry as the guarantee of equality). Differences are then welcomed as the very possibility of synergistic mutual interchange. Where there is bitter dissent and lack of reverence among the three personal constituents of the earthly people of God, there is secular, political struggle and a defaced image of trinitarian love. The image of trinitarian mutuality does not result from human contriving; it develops in graced interchange with the living persons of the Trinity, sacramentalized supremely in the eucharist. For the eucharist is the tangible encounter-point for mutual love: "In the Eucharist we open ourselves to the ultimate presence of the uncreated energies of God along with the personalized acts of the three Persons."[19]

Christian Union with God is a "Real Physical Union"

That being said, there are still unsettling aspects about Cyril of Alexandria's assertion that Christian unity with God and one another is a *real, physical union.* Throughout this study of mutuality we are constantly drawn to ask the gospel question: how can this be, here and now, under our present limitations? It may be facile and reassuring to say that clergy, religious and laity form a trinitarian pattern of relationship. It is more difficult to locate effective examples of such interchange. Moreover, in some areas of the western church it is increasingly difficult to receive the eucharist as the fullest realization of this potential for union. There are several reasons for the obscuring of this vital tenet of faith: 1) for some, there is a tendency to reduce the profound reality of self-gift in the body and the blood to a mere commemoration; 2) for others, there is an overfamiliarity with the liturgical signs and this dulls their participation; and 3) for still others, there is a conviction that presiding at eucharist is a matter of equal rights. When any of these clouds the reality of eucharist, the possibility for imaging perichoretic love is diminished or at times outrightly denied.

B. R. Brinkman's distinction between the "instrumental" and "consummative" modes of sacramentality is helpful here. Christians in the west, says Brinkman, recognize sacramental activity more easily when it is in the instrumental mode, that is, when the body is placed into action for the purpose of *doing* or communicating. Such sacramental activity includes washing, purifying, preparing and blessing food and drink. While this level of sacramental activity is essential, to plateau there is to fall short of the unitive depths of sacramental life, especially the eucharist. To understand this, one need only recall the sixth chapter of John's gospel: Jesus told those who were pursuing him for miraculous bread that they must eat his flesh and drink his blood in order to share his life. Most could not stomach even the thought of this. Or, in Brinkman's terms, they were uncomfortable with the "consummative" mode of sacrament. Consummative modes of action are intimate and unitive. They refer to bodily acts which are innate, such as eating, drinking and genital union.

The *instrumental* mode of sacramental activity can be enacted while maintaining a certain distance from both God and the rest of the community. The *consummative* mode is person-involving and requires an openness to the transcendence underlying Christian sacramental life.[20] It is not a matter of choosing between these modes–both are necessary in celebrating sacraments. It is rather a matter of giving the consummative mode its due. This is especially true in regard to the eucharist, which is not a function to be performed nor an occasion for affirming individual rights. Brinkman emphasizes that sacramental activity is not merely an effort to avoid remoteness:

> It is the most *particular* situation that exists.... So when we wish to express the experience of communion with our God, he has his sacramental body and sacramental blood, and our own bodily contact with him must be by eating and drinking. So with the bodily contact involved in other sacramental actions. It could not be of a more particular *hic et nunc* and tactile variety.[21]

In receiving the risen Christ's body and blood in eucharist, a recipient is brought into contact with the "charter-event" of the paschal mystery and with all previous personal experiences of it. Far from being a neurotic compulsion to repeat, each celebration of the eucharist and each reception of the risen Lord is a love process of deepening communion, bringing about a more integral symbolic reality within the person who enters again and again into that ritual which expresses as no other can the highest possibility of the human person. Because the symbolic content is so highly charged in the eucharist, "the believer is being challenged in the *here and now* experience beyond the point he can cope with."[22] Brinkman notes that even for a person who desires to respond fully to Christ, "precisely what he is doing remains vague to him, and must remain so," because of the immense mystery that is celebrated.

For one who moves constantly deeper into eucharistic communion there can be a disconcerting realization: that in communion with God, besides the symbolism of bodily ingestion, there will also "be present the overtones of sexual union."[23] Now, if the nuptial meaning of body is understood only in genital terms, or if human sexuality is perceived in a distorted manner, a person will hesitate to reflect deeply on the meaning of eucharistic union and find it more comfortable to settle for a "commemorative" interpretation of this supreme sacrament. As we have already seen, the body's basic meaning is nuptial, unitive. Sacramental bodily communication must always be appropriate in degree and scale, but as Brinkman suggests, Christians propose the highest form of religious intimacy possible in the sacraments, and how this "overlaps with cognate forms of human intimacy we have only more to learn."[24] Christ opened to his followers the possibility of living toward ever deeper mutual giving and receiving. Unless the sacred body of the risen Christ is recognized as the center of Christian mutuality, all talk of trinitarian mutuality among laity, clergy and religious will remain polite and brittle. Then, when grave tensions arise, a superficial form of mutuality will be vulnerable to dissolution, like dry bones scattered across the ecclesial landscape.

In the field research conducted for this reflection on mutuality, it was striking that in each community or parish selected for study, the eucharist is a critical factor in their continuing development. As will be seen, when faced with severe challenges to community cohesion, the pastor and parish community of St. Cecilia, Detroit, found it necessary to question their reception of the living body and blood of Christ at a depth far more radical than most parishes ever attempt. Mutuality plumbs marrow and heart.

Jesus' Self-Gift as Food and Drink

Long before Jesus spoke overtly about giving himself as food and drink, he *lived* embodied self-gift in the idiom of Near Eastern daily life. Through that daily repetition of gift he was remotely preparing his contemporaries for the greater gift to come. He spoke the local dialect, lived in a family setting and served as village carpenter. A retreat leader once observed that Jesus spent most of his earthly life "making boxes." The familiar presence of the sacred body of Christ among the Nazarenes was so commonplace–one might say so "instrumental"–that they were baffled when he spoke of opening other levels of his person to them, when he spoke in "consummative" terms. If they could be receptive to that, there was the possibility of introducing them to perichoretic trinitarian love.

Mark reports, however, that "they would not accept him." So long as he stayed within the familiar "instrumental" forms of religion he was acceptable: being faithful at the synagogue; going up to Jerusalem for feasts; and observing the ritual laws that threaded life together. When he began to illuminate the hidden depths within the ordinary it was a different matter.

Jesus' early followers were acquainted with divine interventions concerning food and drink. Their tradition celebrated the gift of manna in the desert, the extraordinary provision of bread and meat for Elijah (I Kings 17:6), and the never-spent jars of meal and oil for the widow of Zarephath (I Kings 17:10–16). When Jesus built on this faith knowledge, some were able to receive a transcendent meaning; others could not make that passage with him. It was never a question of Jesus employing indiscriminate use of power. The gospels of Matthew and Luke narrate how he was tempted to turn stones into bread. Both cite his response: "Man does not live by bread alone." Jesus did not disdain the ordinary goodness of bread, but offered a transcendent nourishment that imparted new value to even ordinary bread. Note that Jesus was tempted not only to satisfy his immediate hunger in a miraculous fashion, but also to turn stone (a creature with its own goodness and purpose) into a convenience that was unsuited to its nature. While Jesus would not violate any being for convenience or personal advantage, *he consistently illuminated and enabled the extraordinary within the ordinary*. He did this especially in regard to the human body and to common forms of nourishment: water, fish, wine and bread.

In his first public "sign" at Cana, Jesus took water in its ordinary potential (to slake thirst, to support vegetation, to cleanse and give delight) and fulfilled that potential far beyond the wedding guests' expectations. In the *ordinary* course of events, water falling on the Galilean hillsides would have sustained roots and caused succulent grapes to flourish on the vines, from which they would pass through the winepress to ferment in new skins. For a divine person, to whom a thousand years are as a day, water, earth, vine and vinedresser commingled at the feast, and guests tasted a wine exceeding their ordinary expectations. At the Cana wedding the immanent presence of the complete giver enabled the ordinary to yield glimmers of extraordinary potential.

In the fourth chapter of John's gospel, Jesus passes through Samaria and requests a drink of water from the solitary woman at the well. When she would have restricted their encounter to a discussion of religious and political barriers, Jesus revealed to her a potential of water that far exceeded the miracle at Cana. Jesus revealed himself as the living water, the divine giver poured out in response to the deepest inner thirsts. This water is able to be a spring inside the recipient and "well up" to eternal life. When the disciples returned with the food that they had procured from the Samaritan village, they were invited to recognize a transcendent food which was still unknown to them: Jesus tells them that he has been nourished by doing the Father's will and completing his work. Through the familiar needs experienced in a noonday desert Jesus opened both the foreign woman and his companions on the journey to the transcendent meaning of food and drink. Respecting their obvious meaning, he drew out their nonobvious potential to express intimate, "consummative" divine-human relationships.

The significance and potential of food and drink became still more evident when Jesus fed the multitude in Galilee shortly before the feast of Passover. In a manner reminiscent of Cana and the Samaritan well, Jesus did not bypass the goodness of everyday food and drink. In fact, he explicitly reverenced and celebrated this goodness, bringing fish and bread into fulfillment beyond anyone's expectations. Because the divine/human giver was present, fish could multiply within a boy's basket as easily as in the dark netted waters of the Sea of Galilee. Without additional yeast, flour or fire, five barley loaves satisfied the hunger of thousands. Increment by increment, Jesus prepared his followers to transcend even these manifestations of the extraordinary within the ordinary. When the multitude sought him on the day after they had eaten the miraculous loaves and fishes, Jesus was very direct in telling them that they had returned for the wrong reason. You "had all the bread you wanted to eat," he said, but you have not recognized the "signs." In citing these Johannine texts within this reflection on mutuality, there is no intent to struggle with precise places, times and numbers, as exegetes and critical biblical scholars must do. The purpose, rather, is to show how Jesus progressively prepared his followers to receive the ultimate meaning of food and drink: *consummate union with him through his body and blood* as a way of entering into perichoretic life, into permanent mutual indwelling. Commenting on the meaning of "bread of life" in the latter portion of John's gospel, chapter six, Raymond Brown writes:

> No longer are we told that eternal life is the result of believing in Jesus; it comes from feeding on his flesh and drinking his blood.... Even though the verses in 51–58 are remarkably like those in 35–50, a new vocabulary runs through them: "eat," "feed," "drink," "flesh," "blood".... if Jesus' words in vi 53 are to have a favorable meaning, they must refer to the Eucharist.[25]

For the most part, those who heard the bread of life discourse found that Jesus' intimate consummative language was intolerable. "How could anyone accept it?" they asked. It was a watershed point in Jesus' revelation. The writer of John's gospel notes bluntly: "After this many of his disciples left him and stopped going with him" (Jn 6:66). Jesus spoke the language of genuine physical union: "My flesh is real food and my blood is real drink. He who eats my flesh and drinks my blood lives in me and I in him" (Jn 6:55–56). Although the promise of such perichoretic physical union scandalized most of his followers, Jesus did not retract his words or reduce them to a metaphor. In fact, he invited the immediate Twelve to make a definite choice. That choice was not rooted in good fellowship or shared work, but in the possibility of a union more intimate than they could have imagined and which transcended all familiar boundaries of food and drink, of body-to-body union. What he placed before them would be realized in the paschal mystery.

Jesus Christ and Mutual Self-Gift

Two aspects of the bread of life revelation are of particular importance in understanding mutuality and in discerning the possibility of perichoretic relations in the church. First, in this revelation Jesus introduced *mutual* self-gift between himself and his own (in eating his flesh and drinking his blood there would be a mutual living within one another, not simply a unilateral giving on the part of Jesus). Second, Jesus shattered the boundaries of ordinary perceptions about eating, drinking, and bodily living within one another. He did this in a multidimensional way, overcoming ordinary limits of space and time right within a space/time world. *He showed that size, quantity and body boundaries are not necessarily limits for being nourishment to others, even living within them.*

What was necessary, rather, was that the giver be truly present in the gift: in the case of the eucharist, to the point of *complete identity* between the gift and its outward sign. He also indicated that living within one another would in turn "draw life" or bring about a "third" from this union. When he reflected on the startling quality of eucharistic intimacy, Benedict Ashley said that "we ought not to think of this merely as the presence of someone facing us in dialogue, but we must retain the fact that he is present to offer himself as our food and drink."[26]

In the technologically astute western nations it is especially necessary to stress the radical nature of the eucharistic and trinitarian intimacy offered by Christ. The living person can now be "disembodied," manipulated and "transmitted" by electronic signals. While the enhancement of personal presence through electronic means is possible, more often scenarios are devised which give the illusion of "real presence," and "photo opportunities" are contrived which distort reality and diminish symbolic reality. In the eucharist, Christ does the obverse, being totally, effectively present despite limitations of size, distance and time. Since the body's meaning is nuptial (unitive) and nuptial gift implicates the total body-person (symbolic reality), Jesus Christ's eucharistic presence in self-gift is the perfect fulfillment of embodied life.

Christ shattered limited understandings of mutuality. Just as he did not denigrate the customary uses of food and drink, he did not disdain the commonplace expressions of human intimacy, but integrated them into a transcendent capacity for union, exceeding all expectations. Even the most ardent spouses, for example, spend only a fraction of their married life in genital intercourse (the temporary, partial living within one another in real, physical union). Yet, "living within one another" is the universal human *vocation*. The eucharist is the paradigm for every embodied mutual exchange. It is the perpetual gift of self spanning all times and cultures: "this is my body given for you." The eucharist illumines why *gift* rather than "substance" or "process" is the fundamental category of being. Process describes the ongoing becoming of a person or being. Processes *serve* that which proceeds or becomes. They carry something forward. In the eucharist, however, the "processes" of liturgical life carry forward a reality that endures: Christ's faithful self-gift. It is the gift rather than the process that is the basic reality.

What then of "substance"? Benedict Ashley says: "The term 'substance' simply indicates that recognizable unity which makes an organism a living system-in-process."[27] The recognizable unity in eucharist is the total Christ offered as gift. In this sense, Christ is "substantially present" in the eucharist. This does not require a precise quantity of matter–only that which is adequate for unequivocally conveying the real presence. "Personal substantial presence" differs greatly within the life of any individual. Although it is invisible to the eye, human life begins at conception and an irrevocable combination of parental gifts determines the unique "personal substantial substance" that exists. Through life there are dramatic changes in size and appearance, but it is the same person who is substantially present. Through the processes of life and death, what is substantially present is the person called to *be* gift. Thus process, substance and gift are not conflicting concepts. The last, *gift*, is the source from which the other two proceed.

Although they seemed to grasp it minimally, the apostles had been prepared for Christ's self-gift as food and drink at the last supper. They had also been prepared to receive new revelation about the perichoretic life of Father, Son and Holy Spirit. At the final meal with Christ they were invited to know this by participation. The gospels baldly relate, however, that rivalry and outright grasping for advantage were manifest at this sacred supper. Throughout their time of formation with him, Jesus had corrected their misunderstandings of discipleship. He had taught by word and example what it meant for him to be in relationship with the Father and the Spirit. This came to a new intensity and tenderness at the last supper, where he attributed an attitude of deference to all three persons. In prodding the apostles to participate in the divine communion of persons, he was also indicating that this attitude of mutual deference should characterize their mutual relations. The washing of their feet was a final preparation so that they might *hear* the revelatory word of perichoresis.

After placing before his readers the question: "Why does the Church exist?" Robert Sears says that the answer lies in the church's being the normative and constitutive embodiment of trinitarian love in the world, "called to realize this love in itself and to cooperate with the movements of grace in the world according to its own experienced knowledge of the community components that enter into that love."[28] For Christians, then, it will always be an aberration to seek "what is one's own" from the church, and to become snagged in power struggles.

George Maloney observes that while perichoresis is the paradigm for union with Christ, it is an element missing from much ecclesiological speculation today. Maloney does not dilute the intensity of the ecclesial call to perichoretic love. The perfection of church unity comes when persons through knowledge and love "indwell one another as do the Divine Persons of the Godhead. Then the Trinitarian model takes on all of its beauty and splendor. If this is true of persons, then it is true of groups of persons, i.e., Christian communities."[29]

The early church had a freedom in expressing forms of divine and human union that many late twentieth century Christians might find questionable. Tertullian, for example, wrote in his *De baptismo:* "Where the Father, Son and the Holy Spirit are, there also is the church, which is the body of the three" (VI). For this reason Leonardo Boff could say in his earlier writing that "the community becomes a figure and analogy of the Trinity," called to make this union palpable to humankind. He pointed to the triad of faith, worship and organization as the means for witnessing or embodying the triune mystery.[30] While I find his triad rather "instrumental," it is helpful in pointing to the *community* as the locus of perichoretic life in the church.

Trinity, Church and Communion of Persons

The trinitarian paradigm applies to the whole people of God, in both universal ecclesial life and in multiple local communities of faith. In order to appreciate the challenges inherent in such an expectation, it is important to enumerate once more the qualities of perichoretic love: 1) mutual self-gift; 2) mutual deference; 3) accord in act and will; 4) co-presence in the missions of other persons; and 5) mutual indwelling. Jesus described perichoretic relations as total self-donation and total receptivity without domination or self-aggrandizement. This is beyond perfect fulfillment for Christians living in a sin-wounded world, but it is always a matter of fruitful tension between the "already" and the "not yet." Immersed in history, communities of faith, like individuals, must move honestly through stages of development. It is not surprising, then, that the church experiences "spasms" of difficulty in attempting to realize perichoretic relations. Within the abiding church, each generation, each culture, each era of human development progresses through unique times of growth, blockage and breakthrough. The abiding, indwelling presence of the Trinity holds the church into its earthly fulfillment despite upheavals within and interpolations from without.

Numerous schemas have been devised depicting the stages of human development–some accent moral growth, others describe psychological or physiological levels of development. Robert Sears has focused on the stages of *spiritual* growth required for transformation by trinitarian love.[31] His schema is helpful in grappling with the hiatus between the vocation to perichoretic love and the often floundering, inadequate attempts to meet that vocation in the church. He presupposes that what applies to the development of the individual applies in a comparable manner to the stages of social development. Thus he looked for parallels in Judeo-Christian history.

The first stage of development is "familial." Impaired as that might be, it is here that the child lays foundations for an integrated personality. The second stage is "uneven," but here the developing person consciously integrates into society even though aspects of the person remain undeveloped or even suppressed. At some point, says Sears, spiritual experience breaks through, requiring transcendence. This is the opening to individuation and a certain universality of spirit. It is the learning to submit to transcendence that takes time and is a long, difficult process, says Sears. The third stage of spiritual development is "incarnational." Here relationships undergo transformation in light of God-experience. *This is an essentially communitarian stage* since relationships cannot be transformed in isolation from a community that is experiencing a similar transformation. Such transformation presupposes a freedom gained during the second stage of development, for genuine relationships are possible only between those who are free and whole. The third stage enables a person to decenter from self for the sake of another–it is a decentering which does not annihilate the self but increases loving understanding and self-gift not only toward God, but toward everyone.[32] In the fourth stage, as a person or community grows in transcending self-gift, there is a desire to extend what has been realized beyond their immediate believing community.

Appealing to Richard of St. Victor's insights regarding trinitarian love, Sears says that a fourth-stage person or community will seek to bring communal love to those who have not yet experienced it.

From his reflection on these stages in Judeo-Christian history, Sears thinks that spiritually, the post-Pentecostal time, or the time of the church is the fourth stage of communal spiritual development. The crucifixion manifested the inadequacy of humanity to represent the fullness of divine love. Only by dying to finite values, immobile self-justification, and limited love will the church reveal the source of its inner life and the call to trinitarian love which is the final goal of the world.

Is Mutuality an Impossible Goal?

It may seem excessive, even pretentious, to hold that trinitarian mutuality should characterize interrelationships within the church. It is not surprising that the meaning of mutuality is frequently diminished or outrightly rejected in light of the difficulties perceived in its realization. This can occur in several ways. First, mutuality is sometimes interpreted sentimentally. Then, in the name of love, "reciprocal giving and receiving" degenerates into a nondiscerning acceptance of human choices and activities, even when they are at variance with the gospel. Differences can be glossed over, as if they did not exist. Second, mutuality is sometimes equated with reciprocal recognition of rights. This reduces the meaning of mutuality to strict justice, a form of *quid pro quo* exchange. Or third, mutuality can be treated with "benign neglect" as a gospel ideal no longer applicable in a world that has radically lost its innocence and must deal with earth-threatening evils. Each of these is a distortion of mutuality. It is important to see why this is so.

The *sentimental* notion of mutuality has strong appeal since it seems to reduce tensions and it obviates the need for dealing forthrightly with conflicting beliefs and values. When that happens, there can be no genuine reconciliation of "incongruities" nor forgiveness of sinful contradictions because their existence is overlooked or denied. Two speakers at the South African Ecumenical Conference in Rustenburg, SA (November, 1990) indirectly dealt with this sentimental notion of mutual relations when they addressed the need for integrity as a prerequisite for Christian unity. John W. de Crouchy said that little would be gained from meeting about "unity" if discussants "failed to speak 'the truth in love' about our divisions, and about the gospel and its implications for us and our witness in society." Any reflection on the church in South Africa must begin, he said, with facing the contradiction that Christians are really divided, fragmented, often in conflict with one another while confessing to be one in Christ.[33]

Speaking at the same conference, theologian Willie D. Jonker said, "Up to a certain point we meet each other to work together, but then move back to our own worlds again, which are not only geographically, but in nearly all other aspects, miles apart." Few cross the color line, he said; very few people know what is going on in Black townships and rural areas. Honest recognition of divisions, together with an expressed longing for authentic union, clears the ground of misapprehensions and allows a "waiting upon mutuality," in which there is no sentimental glossing over of aspects that separate. Forthright acknowledgment of them invites shared prayer and effort until there can be an honest resolution.

The second distortion of mutuality also has a strong appeal today—the equation of mutuality with a reciprocal recognition of "rights." Mutuality *presupposes* justice, but in itself, it is always a matter of love, of self-gift given and received. Efforts to change unjust systems and collaborative work for a new world order based in justice and peace are crucial, but they do not constitute mutuality. If, in the likeness of Jesus, communities of faith risk a mutuality that transcends the level of justice, their imaging of trinitarian love can endure despite radical injustice and mammoth evils that trammel the human community and wound the church from within. Not all who profess to follow Christ will give witness to mutual love. Christ knew this when he revealed the possibility of it at the last supper.

When a faith community searches in isolation for rights, freedom and identity, there can be a shattering of mutual possibilities. An example is seen in the writing of Sharon D. Welch, who stated that she had to distance herself from traditional theology in order to reflect on liberation. She claimed that she could not ground a feminist theology of liberation in either the person and work of Jesus or scripture:

> To do either would be to abdicate liberation theology's uniqueness: its reconceptualization of theology in light of a particular experience of the relation between theory and

> practice. Feminist theology is grounded in the liberating experience of sisterhood.... [W]orking in my particular situation as both oppressor and oppressed has led me to conclusions different from those of black theologians of liberation and Latin American theologians of liberation. The difference lies primarily in our relation to the Christian tradition and in our interpretation of the claim that it is, in some way, "true."[34]

Isolation from the sources of faith, or from the wholeness of the body of Christ brings fragmentation. There is an accord among the mysteries of faith, each of them inhering in all of the others. This is reflective of trinitarian life itself.

A paradox recurs throughout this study: mutuality brings into reconciliation the seemingly incongruous–not by eliminating an other, nor by dominating an other–but by taking those incongruities to their roots with integrity and finding an appropriate means of embodied self-gift and reciprocal receptivity. There is a difference between incongruity and contradiction, however.

For this reason, the multiple divisions and immense evils in society can make the third misunderstanding of mutuality seem the most attractive of all: the rejection of it as an impossible ideal. When that happens, Jesus' words and example are relegated to a remote historical moment: what may have been plausible for a less "experienced" Palestinian people is deemed unrealistic for the sophisticated west poised for entry into the third millennium. While Christ's message may still be inspirational at times, it cannot be taken at face value. It was this assertion that Pope John Paul II countered when he said that "Christ's words are realistic," that they do not attempt to return the human heart to original innocence, but to a "purity of the man of lust" entirely enveloped by Christ's redemption of the body.[35] Pseudo forms of mutual interrelationship will never satisfy the human heart. Nor will it do to turn away from mutuality because it seems to be an elusive ideal.

Jesus Transformed the Meaning of Relationship

Not only did Jesus transform bread beyond anyone's expectations–he also multiplied and transformed the possibilities of interpersonal relationships. The gospels relate particularly how Jesus exemplified this in his relationship with Mary his Mother. From the second century, Mary was termed the "New Eve" in relation to the one whom St. Paul had already called the "New Adam." Epiphanius, writing on the cusp of the fifth century, carried this correlation further, applying the *una caro* or "two-in-one-flesh" union to Jesus and Mary.

Since contemporary society severely limits the meaning of "nuptial" and "two-in-one-flesh" to genital relations, and since familial sexual abuse is so prevalent today, it is important to probe what it *means* to say that Christ and Mary express the ultimate realization of bodily nuptiality and being "two-in-one-flesh," lest there be gross misapprehensions. Once there is initial understanding of this relationship, the possibilities of mutual indwelling within the church will become more apparent. Further, the examples of ongoing struggle for mutual relations which will be presented in the remainder of this book–the communities of St. Egidio and the Sponsor Couples; St. Cecilia's Parish; and the Abbey of Regina Laudis–will take on increased significance in light of the Jesus-Mary relationship. Through his most immediate human bonding with Mary, Jesus was able to *live out* a transformation of relationships between woman and man, between members of a family, and among the whole people of God.

Already at the age of twelve Jesus deliberately expanded Mary's horizons concerning their relationship. Years later, during his public ministry, when Mary came with relatives to visit him, Jesus responded with an instruction on true "relatives." Mark reports that he asked: "Who are my mother and my brothers?" Then, looking about the circle of his disciples he said, "Here are my mother and my brothers. Anyone who does the will of God, that person is my brother and sister and mother" (Mk 3:34–35). On another occasion when a woman from the crowd called out to praise the one who bore and nursed him, Jesus responded, "Still happier those who hear the word of God and keep it" (Lk 11:28). Jesus was inviting his listeners to look beyond their obvious, but constricted, notions of familial relationship. The biological maternal level was good and assured, but Jesus was intent upon opening his listeners to a potential for faithful, transcendent relationships not previously known.

Deeper bonding comes through hearing the word of God and keeping it through doing the will of God. The limited but cogent references to Mary in the gospels are precisely in this vein. "Let what you have said be done to me" is the hallmark of Mary's self-gift in response to divine self-gift. After angels and shepherds departed the place of Jesus' birth, Mary "treasured all these things and pondered them in her heart." Living in God's will and continually opening herself to greater understanding of it characterized her life. Out of this way of life she could counsel the servants at Cana: "Do whatever he tells you." Jesus consistently refused to *limit* his relationship with Mary to ordinary family ties. In so doing, he was addressing the universal call to union and indwelling made possible in trinitarian love. It was through his own Mother that he broke open what it means to be mother, sister and brother.

What is of greater significance, however, is that Jesus spoke of himself as the Bridegroom. By this he indicated his nuptial identity (identity being at the level of person, hence for him, divine person in the flesh). In the gospel of John, it is John the Baptist who first designates Jesus as bridegroom, saying that: "The bride is only for the bridegroom; and yet the bridegroom's friend, who stands there and listens, is glad when he hears the bridegroom's voice" (Jn 3:29). Later, when there was a question of fasting, Jesus said of himself: "Surely the bridegroom's attendants would never think of mourning as long as the bridegroom is still with them? But the time will come for the bridegroom to be taken away from them, and then they will fast" (Matt 9:15).

In the Hebrew covenant from which Jesus emerged, *bridegroom* indicated God's relationship to the chosen people. In their midst he identified with that title. Mary was the pivotal person on whom turned the possibility of bringing the marital covenant between God and people into flesh. Robert Brungs, who has done considerable reflection on the *una caro* relation between Jesus and Mary cites the "Letter on the Priesthood" of Emmett Cardinal Carter:

> It is only in the New Covenant that the problematic character of the relation of the bridal people of God is resolved: only this makes it possible to understand a maritally structured covenant which does not place sexuality in God.... We must stress that Mary's covenantal freedom is created, as the Covenant is. Her created reality is integral with her free affirmation, her conception of the Christ, as his created reality is integral with the free and integral bestowal as

Incarnate, of his Spirit upon her, by which gift she is immaculate.[36]

Mary's conception, free from sin in her mother's womb, was bestowed in anticipation of Jesus' salvific self-gift. There never was a time when she was not redeemed. Although our stumbling attempts at mutuality are always clouded by the sin-condition, Mary and Jesus could know a freely chosen, sinless mutuality of self-gift. This involved intense suffering at times and a human submission to life's uncertainties and all the ravages of a sin-conditioned world.

The nine months of development in Mary's womb constituted the most intense form of indwelling possible in familial life. From the moment of incarnation he received the uninhibited self-gift of the creature, Mary, who provided him with all the inheritance of a human nature, as this was concretized in her family line, within a Galilean milieu. What Jesus invited her (and all who would receive him) to know beyond this body-to-body intimacy was a *permanent indwelling* that was not limited to biological mother and child, but was mutually chosen and open to a "third" beyond one-on-one self-gift.

In what manner can the Jesus-Mary relationship be termed "marital" or "nuptial"? Is this not stretching the relationship beyond its transcendental limits? In order to respond to that, it is important to reiterate that there is a coinherence among all doctrines of the faith–a necessity that they not contradict, but rather mutually illuminate one another. While some doctrines of faith are more central than others (e.g., the Trinity, the incarnation, the paschal event) *no authentic doctrine of faith is dispensable.* That Mary's humanity was integral from the first moment of her conception is critical although it may seem to be of minor importance or merely metaphorical. Because Mary and Jesus were without sin, says Robert Brungs, they were *integral* humanity, the fountainhead of the new creation which could fulfill the vocation given to humanity from the beginning. It is in light of this integrity that one can speak of their being "two-in-one-flesh." Members of the church live in a sin-scarred but sacramental world. Through sacraments we participate in divine life and love. For Jesus and Mary it was not a question of sign or sacrament, but the *reality* to which sign and sacrament refer. For that reason, Brungs says that the integral, spousal union of Christ and Mary does not imply that they were "married":

> Marriage and its sexual expression, is the *image*, the *symbol*, the *sacramental* anticipation of the reality of the two-in-one-flesh unity of the integrally good creation. When we speak of a spousal relationship between Jesus Christ and Mary, we are not speaking of the symbol or of the sacramental anticipation of the reality. We are speaking about the reality itself. Nor is it being stated that the relationship between Christ and Mary is spousal only.... The *una caro* theme, of course, is not simply a spousal image; it is also and clearly a maternal image; it is a Eucharistic image as well.[37]

Jesus did not partake of the eucharist since he is the one given as food and drink. Neither did Mary, since she had never known separation from Christ. This union between Mary and Jesus Christ is "the fullest possible image of the Trinity in a created mode," says Brungs. Mary's maternity cannot do justice to the full reality between the God-man and the woman who knew an abiding two-in-one relationship with him. When Mary stood beneath the cross she was the bonding point between the integral reality and the sacramental community–being simultaneously Mother of Christ and Mother of the whole church, his body. The Second Vatican Council made its own St. Ambrose's naming of Mary as "model of the church." Through her totally human but sinless being, the whole people of God can see their own potential for trinitarian imaging of mutuality in created form. Having even a glimpse of the manner in which both Jesus and Mary lived their bodies nuptially allows contemporary Christians an opportunity to explore what this means in their own relationships, in their own spiritual journeys.

Struggles and Dangers in Realizing Mutual Relationships

This does not preclude immense difficulties for those seeking to live in a perichoretic manner. John Langan enumerates only a few of the struggles and dangers which attend the search for authentic community: self-righteousness, elitism, deviations from traditional faith, worldly alliances, factions and the rejection of authority.[38] New forms of spiritual advance often emerge in the face of opposition. What emerges with fresh life and intensity is often countered from within and without the church. More than that, those whose insights and struggles for interpersonal communion are genuine will welcome the gift of discernment from the larger church, and will endure in spite of persecution. Their strength will come from the conviction that ultimately perichoretic life is what the Christian revelation is about. As Cardinal Joseph Ratzinger says of the fundamental human vocation:

> We are created in the image of God, so relation is our essence, our creational essence. If we are in the image of God this implies two relations. First, it implies that I, as an image, am related to God: relation to God is the fundament of my existence. Second, because God in His own life *is* relation, my own love as expressing God's reality in this world must be relational.... in this mutual condition, one of the relations conditions the other.[39]

What has been said thus far concerning the imaging of trinitarian love may seem highly desirable, even "pleasant." Wherever mutuality is *lived*, however, it will be far from cozy; it will be the very antithesis of a group turned in upon itself. It will require everything: total self-gift and the capacity for receiving the self-gift of others. Jesus' prayer at the last supper, that all be one as he and the Father are one, can actually evoke holy fear in those who understand its implications and recall Cyril of Alexandria's words that this is no mere moral union, but a true physical union. How can this be? Where are the persons and places where mutuality can be recognized, found enfleshed in fresh ways that give credence to Ewert Cousins' assertion that we are at a breakthrough time?

Perhaps the term "model" may be too pretentious when citing examples of mutuality in the contemporary church. We may ask simply if there are examples of persons and communities who emphasize or make visible aspects of mutuality that are meaningful to others and which incarnate the theology of gift which has been developed in this study. Can we find in them analogies for trinitarian perichoretic love, as imperfect and halting as they may be at times?

I would like to focus now on three such areas of life within the church: 1) creative forms of community life formed since the Second Vatican Council; 2) an inner-city parish; and 3) a religious community's faith-rooted relation to the earth. If among them one can find visible expressions of perichoretic love, of interpenetrating exchanges that are faithful and respect the unique gifts of each without domination, then it is possible to say that the theology of mutuality sketched thus far is more than abstract speculation.

Reciprocal Gift in Community

Almost immediately after the Second Vatican Council and its awakening of desire for a spirituality of interpersonal communion, there was a strong impetus among both the laity at large, and those in religious life, to create small, intense communities of faith. Specific ecclesial, cultural, social and economic influences helped to shape these new (or renewed) communities. Despite their variety, they proved to be fresh, common searches for deepened relationships that would result in a more effective faith life. In the now familiar opening of the *Pastoral Constitution on the Church in the Modern World,* the church made its own "the joys and the hopes, the griefs and the anxieties" of this age, identifying itself with the poor and the afflicted in a particular manner. Indeed the document called the church a community "truly and intimately linked with mankind and its history." For many Catholics in the 1960s there was no vibrant, local community life which met this description. Large, unwieldy parishes in some cultures were found to be too impersonal; in the third world countries there was a chasm between rich and poor, despite a common baptism. Since it is difficult to effect change on a massive scale, the renewal of community life began mainly in smaller groups, among those who shared a common vision for renewal of faith life, and who were willing to risk a shared commitment to that vision.

Although the quarter century following the council saw a number of "false starts"—even aberrations—among local groups struggling to form faith community, a number of serious, enduring communities now vivify the church in new ways and they are contributing to a spirituality of interpersonal relations. We will consider only two of these communities: both are lay communities that emerged shortly after the conclusion of the Second Vatican Council. Although their origins, membership, charisms and size are unique, each has maintained a vitality; each has matured in the understanding and living of *communion*. The *St. Egidio Community* began with teen-aged students in Rome; the *Sponsor Couples Community* emerged from married couples along the eastern seaboard of the United States. I have chosen these two from many exemplary, diverse communities because I made initial contact with them shortly after their formation and I revisited them during the course of preparing this work on mutuality.

The St. Egidio Community

The St. Egidio Community was literally founded by teens in a secondary school. In 1968, ten girls and boys, tenth grade students at Virgilio Public School in Rome began to share with one another their disillusionment and lack of meaning in life. Whether they looked at their families, the church, or Italian political life, nothing spoke meaningfully to them. Intuitively, or by unique grace, they sensed that life must have *some* meaning. In a kind of desperation move, they decided to see whether they could find this meaning in scripture. By mutual agreement, they met one hour before classes began, to read the word of God. It was not long before they faced a second decision. Having been deeply "taken" by the gospels, they said to one another: either we have to stop reading, or we must act upon the gospel message. They decided to act upon the word.

As tenth graders they had neither official status nor financial resources. They were aware, however, that Sicilian families had moved north, settling in corrugated iron huts on the outskirts of Rome. The students decided to live their gospel response by visiting the Sicilian community after their classes at the Virgilio, befriending the children and assisting them in their homework.

Soon their peers and observant adults recognized that a change had occurred in the small band of teens. Questions followed: What has made you different? Why are you spending time with the immigrants? Soon some of the questioners were impelled to join them. As their attentiveness to the word of God increased and their outreach to poor children continued, the students began to realize a need for shared prayer and a centering place where they might pray and hold their meetings. In 1973 they began renting an abandoned Carmelite monastery and church in the Trestevere district of Rome. Since the church and its small piazza were named "St. Egidio," the burgeoning group began to identify themselves as "The Community of St. Egidio." Three members of the original band were invited to share their call and experience with members of the School Sisters of Notre Dame at their Rome Generalate in 1976, just eight years after their fragile community beginnings in a secondary school. By that time, two of the trio were completing university studies and the third was in law school. They described their faith journey and their work with the poor. One noted how community members had grown to realize the profound meaning of "church" in ways that far exceeded their adolescent expectations. When asked what continuity could be anticipated as community members completed university work, married and dispersed, one said simply: "Once you *know* this, it is forever, wherever you go." Within the brief eight years of its existence, the St. Egidio Community numbered about seven hundred.

Frequently, when new movements flourish so rapidly, there is a corresponding decline when the first enthusiasm cools. Some fourteen years after the three young men had visited our Generalate and I was doing field research in mutuality, I remembered their witness and wondered if the St. Egidio Community had succumbed to decline, or had grown as a gospel-centered people. *Its emergence had been such an extraordinary example of mutual response to the word of God.*

In October, 1990, I visited the community's soup kitchen and language school in Trestevere, shared in the Saturday evening eucharist at St. Egidio with the founding community and a visiting member group from northern Italy, and interviewed Paola Piscitelli as representative of the community. It was evident that the community had not only survived; it had become a worldwide presence within the church, enfleshing the gospel among the poor.

The "Intuitions" of the St. Egidio Community

Piscitelli spoke of the major intuitions and decisions which have marked the community's development, always returning to its prime intuition or charism–that which has marked it from the beginning: the St. Egidio Community could not claim to be Christian without serving the poor. The parable of the Good Samaritan had been crucial in forming them. Their conviction about serving the poor had been with them from the beginning, but they also knew a necessity to determine *which* poor. When they struggled with that question they felt drawn to the third world, but they made a deliberate decision to serve the poor in Rome, those who were immediately close, yet "far away" from the heart of the church:

> We thought we had to start with those who are near. Sometimes it's easier to say "I love you" because I do *not* see you. I can continue my life without getting involved... when we have to get involved in our relationships, which are daily, "that person" is there and you have to manage with *that* situation. Sometimes the point was simply to learn how to love one another. We didn't know.[40]

Early on, community members recognized their need to learn *how* to be friends. Jesus' first disciples were his friends: he ate with them, spoke and walked with them, grew angry with them! He was trying to build community, Piscitelli said. "Being friends is not natural," she observed, and one of the first realizations of the burgeoning community was this: women and men *could* be friends. Significantly, as Piscitelli spoke of this within the St. Egidio Community, she described growth in friendship in terms of a "third": friendship did not turn in upon the community itself so much, she said, as express itself in learning to build relationships with the poor.

Another "intuition" that guided the community from its early stages concerned politics. While neighboring youth groups thought it necessary to identify with a political party, St. Egidio members made a conscious decision to avoid this. "But why?" reflected Piscitelli: "When we think, who told us? It was our sense, but not ours only. Again, why choose for *these* poor and not others?" She had no facile answers to the questions she posed, but immediately cited another basic intuition. From the beginning, "we had to pray every day." Initially, prayer and scripture reading took place outside the Virgilio secondary school. Now, each evening at 8:30, those who are able to do so, gather at St. Egidio Church for vespers. "We come back in the night because we feel that we need to come back to the Source."[41] This was closely related to another crucial decision, made when the community was forming: *to be within the church.* It was a deliberate choice: the church was the connection with the gospel across the centuries. "We felt free in the church," said Piscitelli, and that conviction of depth belonging has had many ramifications. One concerns the liturgical life of the community. Although they are definitely of the western Roman Catholic Rite, they have incorporated the resonant music and icons of the east into their celebration of eucharist. A few brilliant, strategically-lit icons punctuate the dark interior of St. Egidio Church. "We sometimes think of the Church as a body, breathing with two lungs. So, we need both, the Eastern and the Western. We breathe with both lungs liturgically," said Piscitelli.

This close affiliation with the church is a hallmark of the community. In 1986, the Community of St. Egidio was the first association of the laity to be named a Lay Public Association within the Roman Catholic Church according to the revised Code of Canon Law. Community structures have enabled the original members to remain in communion with one another and to assist in the founding and unifying of other St. Egidio Communities across the world.[42] The Second Vatican Council clarified the universal call to holiness, and the community senses its mission precisely as a lay association in the church. Several ordained priests have joined the community to serve its needs, and several members have been ordained. But, "We are a people of priests," said Piscitelli; we are lay people called to live out and preach the gospel: "Jesus chose absolutely normal people–workers, people with families." The community's rapid growth can be partly attributed to its capacity to adapt to different cultural milieux (Italy, Germany, Belgium, Spain, Hungary, Mexico, El Salvador, Guatemala, Argentina, the Cameroon, Ivory Coast, Mozambique, Bangladesh, Hong Kong, Indonesia). The community maintains a creative tension between a spirit of freedom and an intense, enduring dedication. Although there is no formal profession of commitment, Piscitelli says that community members know clearly who belongs because of the manner in which life is shared, the family sense that unites them: "We know exactly 'who are my brothers and sisters.'"

Personal Relationships Grounded in Scripture and Prayer

Because their founding was so extraordinary–"born in a school," seemingly Spirit-impelled, without the leadership of priests or religious–they were first looked upon with suspicion; but that quickly abated and was replaced by respect. As the community continues its worldwide expansion, new members usually come to join the community through personal relationships: "It's the life itself that teaches you; it's the prayer, the common service and the attendance at meetings," said Piscitelli, who recalled her own encounter with the community as a sixteen-year-old secondary school student. Today, married, the mother of a family, she continues to give herself within the community that is her "life." A physical therapist, she works four to five hours daily at her profession and then serves as principal of the community language school in Trestevere, volunteering her time and service, as do all community members.[43] Like other community members who live in the vicinity, Piscitelli returns for night prayer as often as possible. The community reflects upon its story, she said: "We think that in some way that we do not know yet, the Lord wanted a community like ours in Rome." Pope John Paul II has visited the community on a number of occasions, encouraging their vocation to preach the gospel to those "far away," from the center of church life, particularly the poor and the young.[44] In a brief publication entitled "St. Egidio: What is it?" the members describe their lives:

> The definition of "community," for the Community of St. Egidio, does not derive from a life in common or a sharing of worldly goods, but from the choice of a fraternal and familial life. This choice is expressed both in the sense of spiritual closeness among all its members, and in the offer of communion, hospitality and welcome to everyone, but particularly to the poor, to the pilgrims and to other believers.
>
> The small church of St. Egidio is the heart of the Community's life. Every day members arrive there after a day which has included work and service to the poor. As they listen to the Word of the Lord, they discover that they are humble servants to whom the Lord gives peace and rest.... After the prayer, when people usually go home, they like to stay together for a while talking and eating like a family.[45]

Befriending young children remains vital to the community. As conditions and needs change, works expand: to the handicapped, the elderly, immigrants and refugees, the homeless, persons with AIDS, and gypsies. Community members support their works from their own voluntary contributions, but they seek additional support from friends, schools, parishes and other institutions.

When describing the extent of community works, Paola Piscitelli mentioned another community "intuition": "We never give money to the poor–food, clothing, but not money." She laughed when reflecting upon student beginnings: this "intuition" was a necessity then, since there simply were no funds. The "riches" they had were personal relationships and skills needed to tutor the disadvantaged. "Money spoils the relationship–we are friends," she said. Two things predominate in the community: the word of God, and personal relationships. In "Letters from S. Egidio," published periodically by the Rome community, the columnist assures readers that the community does not judge others according to its own model and option: "We only want to be friends, to live according to the choice of the poor and this is what we have to offer the world." This requires an austere life: "Austerity is an invitation that comes particularly from friendship with the poor with whom we are linked."[46]

Within twenty-three years, the community born in a school has become a world-spanning association, numbering about 15,000, ranging in age from fourteen to one hundred years. Piscitelli says, "We can now consider the Community of St. Egidio as a gathering of different communities." There are aspects of the Community of St. Egidio which illumine mutuality in the image of the blessed Trinity. First, there are the humanly inexplicable origins: that tenth graders would be impelled to take up the word of God, act upon it decisively, and dedicate themselves together, male and female, in the service of the poor defies human explanation. There was a reciprocal giving and receiving among them as friends–but they soon realized that unless a "third," the poor, were included, they could not continue to read the word of God together. In reading the opening chapters of the Acts of the Apostles, they found that the giving and receiving of the early Christian community was as apt for the late twentieth century as it had been for the first disciples. Everything in the community is meant to be "free," said Piscitelli, including participation in prayer. The problem is to do it willingly. "Of course we give to the poor, but we receive," she said, acknowledging her own spiritual indebtedness to those she serves. Archbishop Oscar Romero has been another major influence upon the community. Through his life and death they have come to a heightened appreciation of the links among eucharist, martyrdom, the gospel and love for the poor. The Community of St. Egidio sees love toward the poor "neighbor" as "a love without escaping, being fully involved in the problems, the tragedies, the hopes, the contradictions, in the love of common men and women."[47]

The "Sponsor Couples Community"

This last self-description of the Community of St. Egidio resonates with another small community a continent away–the Sponsor Couples Community in Meriden, Connecticut. Here the "love without escaping," the full involvement in "the tragedies, the hopes, the contradictions, in the love of common men and women," is focused upon the poverty in marriage and family life at the conclusion of the twentieth century. The community was formed in 1970 when three married couples began to meet with members of a post-conciliar religious community, the Franciscan Sisters of the Eucharist, to deepen their marriages and family life, and to contribute to a growing understanding of sexuality within the church. Nearly two decades later, the post-Synod document *Vocation and Mission of the Lay Faithful* would describe such collaboration among the laity and those vowed in religious life:

> Ecclesial communion is more precisely likened to an "organic" communion, analogous to that of a living and functioning body. In fact, at one and the same time it is characterized by a *diversity* and a *complementarity* of vocations and states of life, of ministries, of charisms and responsibilities. Because of this diversity and complementarity every member of the lay faithful is seen *in relation to the whole body* and offers a *totally unique contribution* on behalf of the whole body.[48]

Within the one body of the church, the married couples sought to live their mission in relation to religious and priestly life. At first they were known as the "Married Couples Community," but by 1975, when they realized that mutual commitment was impelling them to reach out to other "thirds," they changed their name to the "Sponsor Couples Community." They "sponsored" persons with particular needs by bringing them into their homes and by sponsoring faith-related events, proper to them as couples and families. The small group of married couples had been impelled to form community through their search for greater depth in their own marriages. In their daily life in the marketplace, they had frequently observed failed marriages, and had experienced a contraceptive mentality that dulled and separated not only spouses, but so much of human interaction. They wanted to understand and deepen their own sexuality, tap the resources of the church, and contribute to a theology of marriage. There is a rich cross-section among the couples in terms of age, professions, and experience. Community membership has been touched by death, and by the choice of some members to withdraw, but the present community of six couples remains small while assisting a number of other specific lay communities to form. Having become acquainted with several of the couples early in the community's formation, I returned to spend several days with them in 1987, the year of the Synod on the Laity. Like St. Egidio members, the Sponsor Couples work closely together, but have their own homes and family life. They also carry out a particular mission from within their homes. Assisted by men and women religious who had the experience of renewing community life following the Second Vatican Council, the Sponsor Couples formulated a set of brief but cogent terms that would form the basis of their meaning as community.

Members make a life commitment to be faithful to one another and to "challenge each member of the Community into becoming what he or she is called to be, but is not yet, in Christ." Spouses expect that beyond their own faithful, deepening relationship, his/her spouse will have other relationships "which are intended to intensify each monogamous marriage and to impel the Corporate community into new inclusiveness." While the community did not formulate their terms in trinitarian imagery, they evidenced from the beginning a desire to intensify their self-gift to one another by incorporating "thirds" within the community, and by reaching beyond their membership. Interviews with couples from the community revealed the richness and the challenge in relationships with "thirds" that have required intensification of their own prime, monogamous commitment.

Community members acknowledge that they have come to grapple more intensely with understandings of interpersonal communion. They value the strength received from community. One woman commented: "I have learned that my spouse cannot be *everything* to me. That is a hard concept because the whole idea in marriage is that you will be for another–and then you realize that you cannot fulfill *every* dimension of your spouse's life! It is much more demanding to live this way ...we are committed to one another for life."[49]

In order to affirm and to practice their call to celibate, communal relationships within a community that strengthens monogamous marriages, the Sponsor Couples choose a woman from one couple and a man from another couple to be the discerning authority among them. Since the married couples formed community in 1970, a number of other small lay communities have emerged, each with a unique focus–either in relation to the Sponsor Couples, or parallel in time of development.[50]

Missions Within a Lay Community

There is realism and earthiness in the way that community members describe their efforts to live out community relationships. They cite with gratitude the value of strong intermarital relationships at a time when promiscuity and infidelity in marriage are so problematic. With human fertility so frequently rejected, or narrowly interpreted in the west today, the couples see the personal witness of their married lives as central to their mission. It is not, however, a mission closed in upon individual couples or the community itself. Each couple has assumed responsibility for a mission uniquely suited to them, and each couple is committed to opening its home to those whom they will "sponsor" in a particular time of need. There is a constant readiness to receive the "third" (who may be sent to them from the religious community that works in close association with them).

Often the very struggles they have known individually or as a couple prepare them to receive persons who are "sent" to them. One mother said of her own youth: "I had done everything by age fourteen and a half, and I mean everything!" When she eventually met the man whom she would marry, each had to face the former infidelities in their lives. Now, as vital members of the community, and young parents, they receive into their own home other young persons who are struggling to achieve a sense of identity. From their own understanding of nonconformity and frustration, they are able to "sponsor" young adults desirous of attaining responsible adulthood. This couple described their mission as "fostering the vital immanence" in those sent to them. By "vital immanence" they mean the "voice" of honesty and depth at the core of the human person, no matter how ugly or distorted that person's life might seem to him/her. The woman acknowledged that she could perceive this vital immanence in others because "that is where my deepest wound is, the hurt is." Together the community members study documents of the church which address marriage and family. They have assumed the responsibility of internalizing an understanding of sexuality and marriage that is grounded in faith–and of sharing this with others. Grappling with the privilege and responsibility of their fertility has led the community couples to reverence fertility with ever deeper understanding. Personal struggles have brought sharp realism to their search. One couple had conceived a child prior to their marriage, while still in their teens; later they had aborted their third child before coming to serious questioning concerning their own fertility, and before they desired to have their marriage blessed. Another couple spoke of their "crisis of infertility" and the "living hell" they experienced. In their struggle, they came into contact with couples who had chosen at some point in their marriage to resolve fertility challenges through surgical intervention–and who now desired to have their sterile condition reversed, and to be life-bearing as couple in numerous ways. So, a new community was formed, of couples attempting to bring their chosen or unchosen infertility into new, life-giving expression. With their support, a communal adoption agency was begun. The Sponsor Couple husband who bears the suffering of natural infertility said:

> We also bring an "empty water pitcher." Our inquisitiveness and questions allow the corporate body to tap into us as infertile.... [W]hen you bring yourself, and allow yourself, like a bride, to be penetrated and "all the wonderful stuff comes out," you hate it and resent it and wish that it had never been discovered. We bring vulnerability, a wanting to know more, but in wanting to know more, to know what we have to give–it hurts sometimes.

Work, within the home and in professions, is an integral expression of community life. Among the members' works in the marketplace are these: foreman of a toolroom; cosmetologist; assistant director of marketing at a bank; speech therapist; and nursing home administrator. One man commented: "What I have learned most from community is to be honest to creation in all that you do, whether it's the way the house is cared for, the way I relate to my children, or the way I work at the shop. People 'pick that up' bodily when we are around." Respect for creation is a lifelong task, he noted, and is "something that you can only do with the help of other people." From a desire to be integral within their living bodies and in all that they do, the community expresses a need in their prayer to be "open to the undisclosed laws of creation."

Living the Lay Priesthood in Community

The meaning of their "lay married priesthood," stemming from baptism, has been a special focus of the community members in recent years, as they discern with greater clarity their own missions within marriage, and the ways in which they are "ordained" or "ordered" within the total body of Christ. They know that this is grounded in their marriages which sign the Christ-church union. A few years ago, their co-authority person, a founding member, died after a brief illness. Reflecting upon that, one man said, "We were fortunate to have had a great lay priest among us in Walter.... As a Community of Sponsor Couples we are grounded in marriage. We study the sacramentality of marriage; we stand for the principles of the Church, seeing intercourse as sacred and life-giving. In the laity, the drive for daily Eucharist and the maintaining of a prayer schedule that is meaningful and fitting for family life are linked with seeing yourself as a sacred person, seeing yourself within marriage as having a call within the Church." His words resonate with the writers of *Embodied in Love,* who say that *all* fully human love is "sexual and passionate, a love in which the lover puts his whole self, including his sexuality and passions, at the service of his beloved, and seeks to promote the whole self of his beloved."[51] The writers distinguish between *promiscuous copulation* and *total sexual love,* saying that in every human action, "entire (sexual) selves" should seek to come into communion with the entire (sexual) selves of all who are met. They add:

> Our nuptial love for all we meet is our wholehearted, passionate concern for, and enjoyment of, each person's distinctive goodness. Such marital love is what God extends to us, his people. Such marital love is what we are commanded to show for each other, as our way of accepting God's love for us. Such marital love is what constitutes the Church.[52]

The Sponsor Couples were challenged to reflect on mutual indwelling through their study of the encyclical *On the Holy Spirit in the Life of the Church and the World.* It was then, they said, that "we discussed ways of relating to the point where you can take each other within yourself, know what it means to compenetrate." When one spouse said "[The] Holy Spirit is the key," her spouse responded immediately that the Holy Spirit is the "answer," the indwelling One who evokes response. There is a Spirit-moment in community, he said. When someone within the community asks, "How do you respond, or *do* you respond?"–that is a Spirit moment. If you are ready, you do–if not, that particular Spirit moment is over. Community touches everything, from family relations to professional work, from raising animals to raising funds for community projects.

In the community interview, there was unanimous acknowledgment of the difficulties involved in such mutual self-giving. One said wryly: "The void of 'no community' is worse than the worst community can get when the challenge gets heavy! Sometimes you don't know how supported you are until you get ten years down the road and look back." In living from a perspective of wholeness, couples take on the burdens of those they serve. A cosmetologist spoke of the intimate service she gives and the manner in which she receives: "Just listening to what their bodies are saying, what they want to pour out to me. Some days I just can't carry more, but I feel that I have something to say in return and I say it." She spoke of ways in which her family takes the "transfer" of this burden from her. In caring for a person's hair, face and hands, there is an intimacy: "It is a very sacred something–that person is entrusting her appearance, her person to you. Whatever comes out of her mouth is part of what she is entrusting. The family all bear that: it reverberates in me when I get home." Coming to realize that authentic love will always incorporate "thirds" (the community, those served, those coming into new, creative relationships) has also meant suffering, because it touches the heart of Christian meaning and spirituality, the paschal mystery.

The community's experience accords with the observations of Wendy Wright, who has studied male-female friendship, and who writes of the maturity required for self-gift that transcends a one-on-one marital bond. There is a creative tension in female-male friendships, a disquieting aspect, heightened she says "by the experience of being drawn so compellingly out of the self by desire." But, she adds that

> by maintaining its own specific life as a friendship and by not becoming either a union of lovers or a marriage or by not retreating into the cool and safely negotiated corridors of an acquaintance, men and women's spiritual friendships come to embody some of the dynamics and gifts of both marriage and celibacy.[53]

The Sponsor Couples are committed to mutual living of such friendships within fidelity to their spouses. They press toward mutual giving and receiving both within their families and beyond, desiring to know better what it means to "indwell" one another faithfully, sponsoring the multiple "thirds" that emerge from their relationships.

When Jesus indicated that doing the will of God made one his brother, sister and mother, He also indicated that among his own (some married, some not) there was a communion that transcended familial lineage. What frequently goes unrecognized is that, except for those covenanted in marriage, *all other relationships are called to be celibate while they are called to be perichoretic.* This is a very human and holy reality. Such love is not learned in isolation. The two communities presented as examples here manifest aspects of that mutual love which has its source and paradigm within inner trinitarian life. They are the leaven within parishes, in the marketplace, and wherever the various "poverties" of the human family are found. But are there *parishes* where such examples of trinitarian mutuality can be found, as incomplete and struggling as they may be?

CHAPTER FIVE

Mutuality in Parish Life

> Grace is relationship. Love is relationship. Eucharist and the sacraments are relationship. The Church is a body of people in relationship. God is a relationship of Three in One. Everything is relationship.... We call our parish "Ceciliaville." I have left my parish [to be here, speaking with you], but my parish is in me. I am related to everything that is going on in that parish.
>
> *–Father Raymond Ellis, Pastor* [1]

The local parish is described in the *Vocation and Mission of the Lay Faithful* as the "most immediate and visible expression" of ecclesial community, and the "place where the very 'mystery' of the Church is present and at work."[2] Since many parishes are based on geographical boundaries rather than established relationships, they can also provide obstacles for realizing a faith community which images trinitarian mutuality. In recent decades, many North American dioceses have adopted policies which either require or encourage priests to accept new assignments after serving several years in a given parish. Priests can then be perceived more in terms of function than relationship. Where faith-centered relationship is considered the basis of parish, and where parish councils are effective and supportive of a full complement of parish-extended services, there are vital communities of faith. How often, though, do parishes witness to the depth of collaborative union described in the *Vocation and Mission of the Lay Faithful*?

> The Church herself, then, is the vine in the gospel. She is *mystery* because the very life and love of the Father, Son and Holy Spirit are the gift gratuitously offered to all those who

> are born of water and the Holy Spirit (cf. Jn 3:5), and called to relive the very *communion* of God and to manifest it and communicate it in history (mission): "In that day," Jesus says, "you will know that I am in my Father and you in me, and I in you" (Jn 14:20).[3]

For parishes to be sacramental signs of trinitarian unity, relationship rather than function must characterize the interchange among laity, religious and priests. Pope John Paul II described the parish as "the place where the very 'mystery' of the Church is present and at work, even if at times it is lacking persons and means, even if at other times it might be scattered over vast territories or almost not to be found in crowded and chaotic modern sections of cities."[4] Simply, he said, a parish is founded on the theological reality of the eucharist. A parish is a "eucharistic community" and a community of faith "constituted by the ordained ministers and other Christians, in which the pastor–who represents the diocesan bishop–is the hierarchical bond with the entire particular Church."[5]

Since the Second Vatican Council, parishes generally have been in transition, experimenting organizationally, socially and liturgically in the hope of building eucharistic communities. In terms of mutuality, the experiment in relational parish life at St. Cecilia Parish, Detroit, Michigan (1965–1971) provided an example of intense search to live the mystery of the church in a nuptial, trinitarian manner. It is notable that this parish was "found in crowded and chaotic modern sections" of a major city, a highly improbable place to find an example of mutuality. It proves especially helpful as example here, since it reveals both the immense potential, and the grave problems which characterize a parish seeking to be a communion of persons.

Shortly before the conclusion of the Second Vatican Council, Father Raymond Ellis was appointed pastor of St. Cecilia, on June 27, 1965. It was a time when Detroit was convulsed by interracial strife and violence. The parish was in swift transition from being a "white Irish parish" to becoming a predominantly Afro-American community. Summer heat was augmented by fires set during racial riots. Twenty-two years later, when I interviewed Rose Ruby, ninety-two-year-old parish sacristan, she recalled vividly the bombings and lootings, and the National Guard stationed in her backyard. She also recalled how the new pastor and his assistant had gone to the bell tower of the church to survey neighborhood destruction and were warned by helicopter personnel to evacuate the tower lest they be shot. After some days the riots had subsided and the work of reconstruction and reconciliation began.

In his first homily, Father Raymond Ellis grounded his pastorate and his understanding of parish in perichoretic union. He said:

> The priest knows his role only if he knows the secrets of God's inner life–and knows the identity of the people he serves. Within the trinitarian life, we observe that each person, Father, Son and Holy Spirit, lives for the other. Each is zealous for the glory of the others. In Christ, we see the Trinity revealed in human expression.... He lives for the glory of the Father and gives His life away for love of us. He came to us to invite us into the trinitarian family of God. He gives us His Spirit to draw us as a family, or as a collective son of God, into the life of God.[6]

The priest, Ellis said, in his installation homily, is taken from the "holy priestly people of God," not losing his identity, but sharing the same basic vocation as all parish members: "[he] must live for others.... There is no meaning to a priest without love.... Just as Christ came to serve not to be served, so too the priest is your servant. The powers he has are for you–not for himself." Everything a priest has, he said, is for giving away. In this opening homily he promised to fulfill the priest's call to be a "public man," whose door would always be open for them. Speaking again from a trinitarian understanding of relationship, he said in the name of the priests serving the parish: "We will live for you so that you will live for each other and all of us will live for God our Father." Most parishioners did not realize how literally he would live the promise to make the rectory an open-door center for them. His pastorate would last almost six years until his sudden death from a heart attack, June 3, 1971. By then, the parish had emerged as a vibrant example of interpersonal communion, despite obstacles, setbacks and imperfections.

Roots, Extensions, Relationships

Addressing priests and religious educators of the Winona, Minnesota Diocese a few months before his death, Ellis described graphically how a shattered people in Detroit came to claim their identity and potential. He spoke with particular anguish since the night before he came to speak, a woman religious, living in the parish convent, had been shot by a sniper's bullet. Although the people of St. Cecilia lived in the police precinct with the third highest murder rate in the United States, Ellis spoke of them as a "joyous, loving community," the most vibrant people in the Detroit archdiocese. Prior to being named pastor, Ellis had lectured in theology and had done extensive work with the deaf community in Detroit. He emphasized that community begins with people learning who they truly are: "If I don't know who I am, how am I going to know who *you* are, who God is?" His approach to helping parish members know their identity was threefold–knowledge of their roots; appreciation for their "extensions"; and the conviction that all exist in relationship. For the parish, this was a concrete, practical approach

Before persons can come into union, said Ellis, each must have a basic sense of identity, a sense of self that is *capable* of giving and receiving. He encouraged parishioners to recognize and claim their rootedness in a family, a people, a land. His parents had emigrated from Lebanon to Detroit when he was very young, and the family lived in an Irish neighborhood. For that reason, Ellis, whose skin and features were vibrantly Near Eastern, spoke with a decided brogue as he served the Black community of inner city Detroit. He would point out the thin, sharp white line around the iris of his eyes, noting that his father and brothers bore the same mark. A medical doctor had told one of his brothers that the white line indicated starvation in the family line within recent generations. Ellis would emphasize to parishioners that each person's body carries the scars and gifts of past generations, marking the pervading roots that each person has within the human family.

With relish he would describe being in Rome when a Lebanese saint was canonized. Ellis had left home at age eighteen, had not heard Arabic for years–but was suddenly immersed in it as he participated in the canonization. "I *understood,*" he said. "It was my mother and my father, the intonations and words from my roots!" For many parishioners, severed from their ancestry, he was a sign of the blessedness of roots, of a specific heritage both wounded and gifted. He enabled their own search.

Together with roots, each person has "extensions." Here Ellis evoked openness to interchange, to the *pre*-catechetical dimensions necessary for understanding a depth call to relationships, in faith. St. Cecilia could not be an inner city island. Parish geographical boundaries encompassed a population between thirty to forty thousand people, few identifying themselves as Roman Catholic; many were Muslim; some belonged to other Christian denominations, and a good number had no perceptible faith identification. The parish extended into every aspect of life and needed to cope with barriers resulting from violence, suspicion, sometimes outright hatred.

A conscious decision was made in two aspects of parish life: 1) it would retain an unambiguous Roman Catholic faith under the apt patronage of the virgin and martyr, St. Cecilia; and 2) it would extend itself and its services into the larger community. To sign both of these in a concrete manner, the parish began to identify itself as "Ceciliaville." In order for the faith community to plan projects, and to grasp the location and circumstances of parish members, a large relief map of the entire parish was constructed in the rectory basement, depicting homes, commercial areas, highways and public buildings.[7] Comprehensive planning was done, involving appropriate collaborators within and beyond the parish.

Among the projects which expressed the parish in its extensions were the music festivals, the tool skills learning center, year-round sports center and extensive educational programs, including the parish school. When the parish became known for its vibrant life, Father Ellis was invited to speak in other dioceses. Whenever possible, he did not go alone, so that the parish could be represented in its variety of persons and gifts. When he did go alone, he would report to his parishioners in the weekly parish newsletter, *The Beacon*. After such a journey in 1968, he wrote to his parishioners:

> I spoke as pastor about Ceciliaville. This is my home. You are my home. I explained how we had the model of Ceciliaville on the parking lot last summer during the music festival and how excited the youngsters were in trying to locate their homes. A person must have some stability. He must live some place and the more defined that place is, the better. That is why we have Ceciliaville. It is a small place in this huge sprawling metropolitan area where we can say we are "at home." Our home goes far beyond

> the skins of our bodies. Everything that enters us and finds a home in us becomes our home as well. Everything we breathe or see or hear or touch or taste; this is our home. The smoke is our home. So, too, are the garbage cans in the alleys, the sound of autos, the smell of good food cooking. All this is where I live and all this lives in me.[8]

"Choosing One" Means Choosing All

The parish extended into its environment, touched by all of its problems and potentially destructive elements, in order to bring them into redemptive interchange. Liturgies, social programs and teaching at Ceciliaville were premised on an understanding of *choice* which sprang simultaneously from incarnational theology and an honest acknowledgment of created reality. The community was invited to reflect very simply and directly on its own experience in light of faith. Utilizing the teaching method of Jesus, Ellis taught from the commonalities of life (which for most people in Ceciliaville meant struggling with skin color, family life, small threatened patches of grass, garbage, broken windows and deteriorating plumbing). Instead of focusing upon a feeling of helplessness and disadvantage, he stressed the possibility of *choice* in dealing with these extensions.

Foundational to that was an understanding of what it means to "choose *one*." To really choose one means to choose all. "If I choose you," he said, "I have to choose your roots, extensions and relationships."[9] He used the simple examples of peanuts and apples to illustrate the point. If you have a bowl of peanuts, can you choose only one peanut? he would ask. By the manner in which you eat and relish one peanut, you are saying that you like peanuts, *all* peanuts. Similarly, to eat one apple with delight, to respect it, expresses an attitude toward all apples. There is a wholeness in the universe: the manner in which *one* aspect is chosen, received and reverenced touches all. Another example that Ellis used was a carpet. The unfaded, unsoiled portions in the corners or under the sofa cannot say to the soiled, downtrodden portion by the door: I have nothing to do with you. Spilling paint on a hidden portion stains the whole carpet, interwoven as one piece. Using concrete terms such as these, Ellis helped the parish reflect on its extensions and interwoven life.

Parishioners were encouraged to realize that truly choosing *one* person meant choosing the entire universe. Although he did not explicitly refer to the trinitarian theology of Richard of St. Victor, Ellis said that genuine love required the lover's desire that all others respond lovingly to the beloved. Whatever endangered, whatever prevented growth or caused unnecessary pain was of concern to the lover, who desired only the good of the chosen one. The chosen one needs clean air to breathe, requires beauty and safety in the environment, and needs opportunities to become all that he/she is called to be. Ultimately, to choose one involves choosing the good of the entire universe. Ellis reflected:

> There seems to be built into the word "choice" its opposite–rejection. Does choice of one imply rejection of all others, or is the opposite true? The crisis is not to love everybody. The crisis is this: am I able to really love *one* person...the problem of white people who hate black people is not that white people can't stand black people, but white people can't love white people either. When you have a black man who hates all white people, he doesn't love black people, either. It's his inability to extend himself to even one other person.[10]

Similarly, when God chooses one–all are chosen. When God chose a particular people, it was a sign of all being chosen. In taking on one humanity, God was choosing all humanity, its roots, extensions and relationships. "When the Father opens himself to man, he opens himself to all that is implied–the universe," said Ellis. The choice of Jesus does not mean the rejection of everything else, or "all the little words." Each human being is a microcosm, so in embracing *One*, God embraces the universe.[11]

This approach was not theoretical in Ceciliaville. Parishioners were invited to contribute personal talents, to specify "choices of one" that would build the parish and extend into the larger community. The Neighborhood Youth Corps (an employment program) was begun, along with extensive athletic and scouting programs. The annual music festival brought musicians and dancers from the larger Detroit area. The Skill Center, supported by companies where parishioners worked, allowed residents to learn plumbing techniques and other skills for home improvement. The school became a focal point for life-education. Projects such as the Neighborhood Youth Corps were based on theological principles celebrated in the liturgy. The pastor worked alongside youths learning seemingly menial tasks. Since garbage was a major offense to the humanity of the inner city, Ellis taught the young men that the parish hired, to see the dignity of garbage disposal. Working with them in cafeteria or alley, he would reflect how coffee grounds, grapefruit rinds and eggshells in the garbage represented a gift that had been received and enjoyed. In the context of Philippians 2, which celebrates Christ's self-emptying, he taught that the remains of food represent gifts of the earth poured out in complete self-gift. The way to be thankful is to give them a "decent burial" by packaging them properly and then cleansing the containers "so that your nose is not offended by them." Ellis became known familiarly as the pastor with a "theology of garbage." What happened in the proper maintenance of parish property had direct reference to the celebration of eucharist, since life was "all of one piece." The summer prior to Ellis' appointment as pastor, all the school windows had been shattered. Three years later he reflected that only three windows had been broken that summer—all accidentally, and all had been reported.

As parishioners grew in their understanding of their interrelatedness with material surroundings, it was possible to touch at deeper levels the personal, bodily racial issues involved in identity and choice. A parishioner whose talents and self-gift contributed significantly to the melding of theology, art and life is DeVon Cunningham, artist and a vice president at Detroit Edison. When I interviewed him some twenty years after he had painted the "Black Christ" in the apse of St. Cecilia Church, he spoke of that experience, and the principles that prompted it. He also spoke of the destructive violence in the 1960s and its impact on religious belief. School children, including his own daughter, had burned religious books on the playground of the parish school during racial turbulence in Detroit.

The "Black Christ"

In the wake of violence, Father Ellis asked Cunningham if he would paint a "Black Christ" in the apse of the parish church. Cunningham vividly recalls how pastor and artist stood together in the church, struggling with the possibility. The pastor had pointed to the impressive "White Pantocrator" that graced the apse, surrounded by "white cherubs," and said that Black people entering this place of worship had no visual images to express their identity and heritage. He and Cunningham grappled with the theology underlying the artistic representation of a "Black Christ," and the feasibility of carrying out the project. Cunningham said that he had resisted because "I didn't know how Christ looked, and I didn't think I could paint a Black Christ up there. I wouldn't dare." Then Ellis opened scripture to Jesus' saying, "I am the vine, you are the branches," and "you are in me and I am in you" (Jn 15:5; and 17:21). Ellis said:

> What you are going to paint is not the historical Christ. You are going to paint the Risen Christ, the one who came back in the Spirit, in all.... He is whatever color humanity is. He said "I am in you and you are in me." So, once you have accepted Christ and you are baptized and Christ is in you, you receive Christ. You receive him within yourself. Not with a gene, or cell or blood transfusion, but in the Spirit.[12]

Father Ellis contributed his meager life savings to the erection of the scaffolding needed for the artist's work in the cathedral-like sanctuary. DeVon Cunningham is terrified of heights and was unsure of ascending the scaffold once it was in place. "Once I got up, I tied myself with ropes. I was so scared I could hear the scaffolding shake. I told them they could bring my food up!" Cunningham recalled. He began to paint.

In his weekly column in *The Beacon*, the parish newsletter, Father Ellis would later write: "DeVon himself confessed that the Spirit painted the face of Christ for him. He did not make one misstroke. In just a few hours he had the face perfect. And this, in spite of the fact that he had himself tied to the scaffolding by ropes and held on to the railing with one hand as he painted with the other."[13] Cunningham portrayed angels as vigorous beings, bearing features of different races and people of color. Along the bottom of the huge painting he created a mural depicting the Detroit skyline in cloud, interspersed with faces of twentieth century persons who have contributed significantly to human becoming. A theology of color underlay the work. The "Black Christ" was a visual way of expressing every person's relationship with Christ, and every other human person. Celebrants for the Easter Vigil at St. Cecilia in 1968 wore a mix of white and black vestments, Ellis saying:

> Resurrection can be any color. When Christ rose from the dead on that first Easter morning, his humanity was completely drawn within the life of the Trinity. His humanity was totally absorbed within the life of God. His, now, was an entirely new mode of existing as a human being. His was a life now of undreamed splendor and power. This was resurrection. It can be any or all colors. Black is any color and at the same time it is all colors. Black is total absorption. All the light rays together make up the color black. So, resurrection can be symbolized by black.[14]

Both artist and pastor received threatening telephone calls and vituperative written messages (some of which were published in *The Beacon*, allowing the parish as a body to share misunderstanding and hatred). A brick was thrown through the front window of the Cunningham's home.

Receiving others, together with their roots and all of their extensions is necessary for the ultimate call of human life: relationships. Ultimately, the parish of Ceciliaville was to realize in all of its woundedness something of the prayer of Jesus in the last discourse. Mutual indwelling was a theme that pervaded the liturgies, teaching and projects at St. Cecilia. First communicants were reminded that they not only received the body and blood of Christ–but one another. Ellis told them: "I live in you! I must, because your eyes are *you*, and when your eyes are open, I am going right inside of you. My image flashing on your retina and your mind make a conversion of that and you have *me!*"[15] Tirelessly the pastor reiterated the basic principles of mutual union. Between him and his parishioners there was an invisible bond, and he was keenly aware how he bore the parish within him. "To touch me is to touch my whole parish," he said. Father Ellis had a nuptial theology of parish, flowing from the nuptial meaning of the church in relation to Christ. He wrote to his parishioners:

> To be at home with and in Christ is to be at home with and in you. Separation from you means to be separated from

> Christ. Since Christ and you are one, head and body, then together you and He make up my way to the Father's home.... Every time, as the Pastor of Ceciliaville, I receive Holy Communion or preach the word or do any other salvation action, I come into deep union with my people. I make my home in their hearts and they make their home in mine. It is like a marriage union.[16]

Leaving the parish to give a retreat to Franciscan priests, Ellis wrote that he would carry the parish with him: "It will be a Ceciliaville retreat. The Franciscans will come to know and love you very well because they will see that we are one."[17]

The Bread of Life and Mutual Receptivity

There was also a frank admission of failures to "make one." One evening each week the liturgy committee, together with any other parishioners or guests who desired to join them, were invited to meet and "contemporize" the scripture readings for the coming Sunday. From the dialogue, Ellis would shape his Sunday homily, attributing major insights to parishioners who had participated in the "contemporizing." In the summer of 1970 the committee was pondering the bread of life discourse from John's gospel. The pastor arrived late, looking worn; he asked what had been shared–and then told the group that he could not give a homily on the bread of life the following Sunday. He went on to describe the struggle he had with a young man that the parish had hired to clean the school floors. As was his usual practice, Ellis had worked with him, had taught him how to use the equipment for washing and waxing the floors. When Ellis returned later, the youth had simply waxed over the unwashed floor. Ellis again explained the process, left, and when he returned, found that the same abuse of equipment and floors had occurred. Ellis told the liturgy committee: "I told him to leave, to get out! *I could not stomach him.* Until I can stomach that young man, I cannot preach on the bread of life." Those gathered to reflect on the gospel assured him that his anger was appropriate and the dismissal necessary. Nevertheless, on the following Sunday, the pastor confessed his inadequacy to the people. It was consistent with his catechesis to the first communicants. "I am going to eat you," he would tell them, because in receiving the body and blood of Christ, I am receiving you also.

Parishioners were invited to entrust their lives to God and to one another, and the pastor entrusted his life to them. "Jesus is the Father's embrace of the whole fabric.... The first thing you know about every man is that he is locked in with you."[18] Trinitarian relationships were seen as the basis for reconciliation and love between people of different races:

> God is three persons, each one living for the other. Love is possible only when there is the other. Love is impossible when there is only one. God is three persons. Otherwise it would be impossible for God to be Love. The whole idea of our Christian faith is that God wishes to bring man into this love relationship which God is. The whole of religion is love relationships.[19]

This required a parish given in service; so, assistant pastors and many people who asked to come for pastoral experiences at St. Cecilia shared with the parishioners in a variety of works.[20]

Father Raymond Ellis died suddenly at age forty-eight, not quite six years into his pastorate at St. Cecilia and the experiment of developing parish life within the nuptial mystery.[21] Overflow crowds participated in the funeral mass for this priest, buried symbolically in black vestments. Young Black acolytes broke rank to crowd about the hearse, knock on its windows and plead, "Don't leave us." Black and white shared mutual grief. In "Life, Death and the Theology of Garbage," it was said: "Ray Ellis was an extraordinary man. He moved people. He made them conscious of identity and mission. If our times have produced a single priest-prophet, it was he."[22]

Brilliant Witness, Imperfect Realization

Ceciliaville emerged with intense brilliance after the Second Vatican Council. What endured? I returned to Detroit sixteen years after Father Ellis' death to speak with parishioners, as well as with men and women religious who had been associated with St. Cecilia in the time of intense experimentation. One woman reflected, "We were allowed to be ourselves in the church, to be who we are." A woman religious spoke of the self-giving that had occurred, but also of the inadequacies inherent in human efforts to live a trinitarian-based community. There had been misunderstandings–serious misunderstandings about the "Black Christ"–and misunderstandings about small matters, such as placing the offertory collection on the altar as sign of the sweat and toil of the week, offered with Christ. After Ellis' death these struggles surfaced. What was needed, one person commented, was for someone to take that mode of operation and extend it: "I feel that he certainly hasn't died for me, but that he is in me. You talk about indwelling. He was formative of my understanding, certainly of the eucharist." Citing the immense challenge in a parish transformed from an Irish ghetto into a predominantly Black community, a priest who served at Ceciliaville after Ellis' death acknowledged the immense problems that attended the striking witness of Ceciliaville. He noted that Ellis saw the far-flung parish in terms of concentric circles: anyone could move as close as they desired to the center, depending on call, response and desire. The hope had been to form a core of persons committed for life to the intense mission of Ceciliaville within the church. This would have been a stable, holding core, but it needed a priestly complement. When Ellis died, neither the core of committed laity nor priestly core in complement had been realized to the extent that it could long survive. The profound, nuptial understanding of church which Father Raymond Ellis brought was not shared by most priests. "When he died, the relationship died because there was no body of priests to pick it up," observed a priest who ministered at St. Cecilia after Ellis' death. He said:

> For some who watched this post-Council experiment, it seemed oppressive. Father Ellis knew the Trinitarian mystery and that is why it worked. When you don't have this capacity you need other forms so that it *doesn't* become oppressive.

Ellis died, in God's providence, before the Black nucleus of the parish had been formed in its mission/commitment. Maybe that was better, the priest observed, since there was no priestly complement formed yet, either. Ellis had made a consistent effort to prepare Black men for priesthood; he desired to have men ordained who understood the Black experience from within, and who knew a union between liturgy and life. Many who were committed to social justice saw a dichotomy between formal liturgical services and the concerns of social justice. The unified approach of Ceciliaville seemed suspicious to them. In the late nineteen-sixties and early seventies some within the church were advocating the selling of church buildings, in order to translate the money into food and clothing for the poor–seeing the liturgy as irrelevant. For Ellis and Ceciliaville, it was not a matter of "either-or," but "both-and." In the funeral homily, preached by his friend, Father John Markham, Ellis was shown to be a man of suffering. Markham chose the gospel text John 21:15–18, in which Jesus tells Peter that he will stretch out his hands and be taken where he would rather not go. Markham applied this to Ellis. The pastor had been known for his loving care of the deaf, for his fluency in "signing":

> But you do not know, and you should know, that he would rise early; he would sign into a mirror; he would then go into the bathroom and lose his breakfast. And he would say to me, "Johnny, I can't do it." But he did. He went and followed the Spirit where he otherwise would not go.[23]

Numerous forms of experimentation in parish community life have been attempted since the Second Vatican Council. The "Ceciliaville experiment" is unique in its attempt to live the principles of inner trinitarian life under the most trying of social circumstances. Joseph Fox said in his study of St. Cecilia Parish:

> Fr. Ellis was trying to make the mysteries of the faith come to life in his people. He wanted them to experience the depth of relation to God that is revealed in Scripture in the nuptial imagery. In order to bridge the gap between the scriptural image and the life they lived in the third highest crime district in the country, he had to develop a sense of corporate body among his parishioners. He wanted them to see the day when out of their own midst ministers would be called to ordained service among them as a local community of believers.... [This] leading his people into a nuptial relation with God through the Church was not without failures.[24]

Like the vision of Charles de Foucauld that remained dormant for decades after his death, the vision of Father Raymond Ellis concerning the nuptial mystery in parish life may await others to bring it to lasting fruition.

CHAPTER SIX

Mutual Relations with the Earth

> The *spirit* of the earth is the spirit of creation itself, the potential placed in it by God to evolve toward God. The spirit of the earth is a reflection of God's immanence, of the Spirit of the earth; it is also an indication of God's imminence as ages pass and creation strains toward God, strains to have the spirit taken up into the Spirit: "All creation groans and is in agony" (Rom. 8:22) waiting for that ultimate union.
>
> –*John Hart* [1]

The two previous chapters have explored aspects of perichoretic mutuality in small communities and parish life (as partial and wounded as these may be). Is it possible to experience mutuality with non-personal creatures, with all of creation, which St. Paul described as groaning and in agony until ultimate union is realized? Throughout this study it has been affirmed that the entire universe bears the pattern of the Trinity in a variety of analogous ways. Nathan Wood goes so far as to say that this is "self-evident," and that the universe is "one vast evidence of that triunity of Father, Son and Holy Spirit in God."[2] He asserts that God's triunity explains the universe since it is the organizing principle of all things and verifies the claims of Jesus. Far earlier, Thomas Aquinas wrote that all three divine persons participate "in the single act of creation." Creation does not refer to some "generic" triune God, without distinction of persons. It refers to divine persons in relationship. As Leonardo Boff points out, there is a trinitarian character to creation, "and being trinitarian is being in permanent perichoresis."[3] If creation is trinitarian in character and is "in permanent perichoresis," it has immense dignity, deserving of profound reverence. "For Paul," writes Joseph A. Fitzmyer, "the created physical universe is not to be a mere spectator of man's triumphant glory and freedom, but is to share in it."[4] The Father creates through the Son, *in* the Spirit–thus the Holy Spirit is ever active in creation. While the "work" of creation is primarily appropriated to the Father, the entire Trinity shares in it and is mirrored in some fashion within it. To the Father is attributed the mystery of creation; to the Son all that is reason, logic and wisdom in creation; and to the Holy Spirit all that is love, gift and integration. All creation is "a majestic sacrament of the Trinity."[5]

This trinitarian immanence in all of creation is not "Christian pantheism." Rather, it presupposes divine transcendence, just as it presupposes the distinction between personal and nonpersonal creatures. In fact, only within that basic understanding is it possible to speak of integral *relationship:* a union which is appropriate and respectful of each, while maintaining distinctions. It is helpful to recall Martin Buber's clarifications regarding the different stages or levels of mutuality–particularly those levels regarding personal mutuality with nonpersonal beings. Among Martin Buber's writings on mutuality, it was the realm of the nonpersonal that most troubled some readers. Buber maintained that "relation is mutuality" and "mutuality is reciprocity," but

> applied literally to the nonhuman, such a locution will always be confusing. For what Buber wants and needs to say is that it is in our relating attitude to other things and beings that we become persons, not that the other thing or being becomes a person, unless he or she is human. There is no need to personalize the nonhuman things and beings of the world in relation to which we find our own life as persons occasioned.[6]

Buber was convinced that an "I-You" approach to *every* being was transformative of human existence. Therefore, in contemplating a tree, in *encountering* a tree as "You," Buber found a reciprocal relationship which included not only its form and mechanics, colors and chemistry, but also "its conversation with the elements and its conversation with the stars–all this in its entirety.... What I encounter is neither the soul of a tree nor a dryad, but the tree itself."[7] The distinctions of this contemplative philosopher assist in clarifying the degrees or levels of mutuality.

Perhaps there is less danger of deifying nonpersonal creation today than there is of devastating, even annihilating major portions of it. Current technological capacities for destruction eclipse all previous atrocities committed in regard to the earth. Images of Hiroshima's ruins and of Kuwait's torched oil wells have burned into the twentieth century consciousness. Majestic cranes and seals, wallowing in oil spills, besmirch memories of coastal waters. The groanings of creation have never been so evident. The media are awash with slogans advocating multiple ways of "saving the earth," with environmental programs bent on restoring what has been abused. Various motives prompt such earth-saving programs. Some are aimed at the sheer survival of species or resources—or even the survival of the human race itself. While these are praiseworthy, to a degree, they do not touch the profound vocation given with the act of creation. In Boff's words, "The whole of creation is a majestic sacrament of the Trinity." The earth is a wounded sacramental reality, bearing the marks of sinful humanity, but nevertheless brought into existence as part of a divine cosmic plan, and already caught up in the one act of redemption.

Within the church, especially since the Second Vatican Council, there have been consistent efforts to reawaken awareness of the sacramentality of creation, and to take practical measures that ensure stewardship and care of the earth. These efforts have been spurred by encyclicals, international and regional conferences on social justice, as well as major pastoral letters on economics, care of the earth, and the development of underprivileged nations. As in previous chapters, the intent here is to focus on *examples of lived mutuality*—in this case, a mutuality with the earth that is rooted in an integral faith perspective.

Life Becomes Abstract Apart From Contact with the Land

Among excellent examples, I have chosen to focus on mutuality with the land as concretized at the Abbey of Regina Laudis, Bethlehem, Connecticut. Within the approximately fifteen centuries of Benedictine tradition, this abbey is of recent founding, having been established in the rolling foothills of the Berkshire Mountains shortly after the end of World War II. From the abbey's inception, however, the foundress, Lady Abbess M. Benedict Duss, knew that (contrary to the common practice in twentieth century western monasticism) it would be essential for the new foundation to maintain vital contact with the land, since losing this contact would result in life itself becoming abstract.[8]

Once more, in citing the Abbey of Regina Laudis as an example of mutuality with the earth, it is important to reiterate that human attempts at mutuality are always limited, partial. Nevertheless, the abbey is a striking example of perichoretic mutuality with the earth through 1) a conscious, deliberate effort to integrate liturgical prayer and life with the land and all of its extensions; 2) concretization of this effort in the practicalities of daily life; and 3) an approach to creation that is rooted in the incarnation. These three aspects are interwoven as the community chants the divine office, labors on the land, and re-creates in the late twentieth century the Benedictine tradition of art and learning. This integration characterizes the abbey's manner of receiving guests and of working with young adults who come from various nations to participate in the abbey's land program. The abbatial community understands that the impetus and energy for their form of life flow from consecrated virginity. What occurs in the land programs at the abbey derives from the "dedicated land" of their own lived bodies. (It was at Regina Laudis that the *Consecratio Virginis,* a sacramental conferred by a bishop, was solemnized for the first time in the United States.)

Abbeys which hold the origins of the Benedictine tradition remind visitors of St. Benedict's integral vision: for example, there is an "at-home-ness" with the earth sacramentalized in the frescoed caves of Subiaco, and starkly marked by the "rock of miracles" beneath the reconstructed Abbey of Monte Cassino. Familiarity with rock and soil is becoming rarer, nevertheless, even among Benedictine monasteries. This makes Regina Laudis' approach to the land all the more striking. While the abbey community writes sparingly of itself, their annual Christmas card is a cryptic faith summary of the previous year's work and prayer. The cards are twofold, having a strong visual image which characterizes the major abbatial focus of the previous year, and a tightly-knit essay, linking that image to the community's life.

For example, the 1974 card celebrated the initial expansion of the abbey on Burritt Hill, a pine-covered fifty-acre tract of land given to the community in 1946 by Robert Leather. That year work had begun on a circular tower, constructed of New England fieldstone.

Two lay communities of young adults associated with the abbey had constructed by hand the stone archway that would one day serve as entry to a circular chapter room. The image on the 1974 card was that of the Roman arch which spans the courtyard at Benedict's Subiaco, in Italy. The accompanying essay linked that arch ("seminal shape of Benedictine monasticism") with the covenant rainbow, the maternal womb, the bird's rounded nest–but also with the rolling Connecticut hills, the undulations of Gregorian chant, and community relationships which have "the roundness of joyful exchange, made of a subtle blend of dignity, freedom and trust; a mutual covenant girt by the radiant *communio sanctorum* of the cenobitical life." When the ancient manner of constructing an arch is employed, wooden supports undergird the placement of rocks and mortar. When the arch is completed and the mortar has "set" for several hours, the wooden frame is removed. If the construction has been carried out correctly, each stone "groans" as the entire structure moves "the infinitesimal distance" to a final position, "releasing the pure and emphatic curve of the arch." When the abbatial and lay communities gathered for the removal of the wooden form on Burritt Hill, the arch held and "a tumult of joy broke loose." It was not simply the completion of an art form: it was the integration of earth, community, prayer and labor. The Christmas essay expressed this:

> When the thrust of an arch, when the spirit of an arch is thus felt in body, one is impelled into the desire to understand something of the mystery involved in the capacity the arch has to soar. The same weight existing in a pile of unrelated stones would simply press further towards the center of gravity. But in this kind of structure, where rock and mortar are organically interrelated, a new form of energy becomes operative. The arch's weight must be considered in relation to its depth: the deeper the arch, the greater the pressures.... By analogy, an aggregate of persons would unquestionably generate a certain amount of energy. But true community organically interrelated–though the membership quantitatively and qualitatively might appear insignificant–will yield immeasurable thrusts of energy of which we might be unaware, as we would be in considering

> the arch did we not labor to understand something of the mystery of its soaring.[9]

By 1989 a novitiate building had been erected near the archway (by then an entry to the nearly completed chapter room). That year the Christmas card celebrated frescos from the Abbey of San Vincenzo, Volturno, Italy: The Annunciation and The Hand of the Father. It was the year that members of the Regina Laudis foundation began restoring monastic life at this ancient abbey near Monte Cassino.[10] The Christmas essay dwelt particularly, however, on the novitiate at Regina Laudis. Despite constricted living space in the original abbey buildings (converted mainly from a former small brass factory and a barn), the community had waited almost half a century to build the cedar log structure. Their patience extended beyond economic considerations. Why wait for so long?

> The answer lies within the Theology of Architecture in which we have been formed: our architectural structures will only be authentic insofar as they reflect and embody personal structures of our community life, individually and collectively.... We build on the rock–the extensive granite slab deep below Burritt Hill–which mirrors for us the Rock of Christ in the Church.[11]

Unearthing Theological Insight

At Regina Laudis, the bond between liturgical prayer and land is forged through the practicals of daily monastic life. The community not only ponder and pray over the connections, but speak of cherishing the opportunity to know the contours of Burritt Hill: here they utilize chain saws and wood chippers to clear trees and tangled underbrush surrounding the buildings in the New England pine forest, preparing the way for an abbey church. Hands-on work unearths theological insight, which runs like electricity among community members and the New England stone walls and arches (which are the striking motif of abbey buildings and enclosure walls). Grappling with the underbrush does not mean a naive "back-to-the-land" retreat from the urgent world-encompassing issues which the church as a whole is called to address. The invitation to restore the ancient monastery of

San Vincenzo, for example, was described in the 1989 Christmas card as "opening widely to the ever-successive terrors of the mystery of the Incarnation and which are named today 'enculturation,' 'evangelization,' 'mission,' all of which nonetheless invigorate through Holy Fear the stronghold for multiple deaths."[12]

The abbey's approach to the earth resonates with Leonard Weber's distinction between "working with" and "using" land. Inherent in a "partnership of land ethics," says Weber, is an implied respect for the fundamental nature of the land. This means an *interchange* that does not destroy its nature and which returns "something of value in exchange for its use."[13] Aware of relationships among body and earth, life and prayer, the abbey community is attuned to the natural rhythms of the body, the seasons, the animal and vegetative life on abbey land. In making the foundation, Abbess Duss was convinced that anyone seeking entrance into the abbatial community should be grounded in a profession, a field of study or area of expertise suited to her personal gifts. Without such grounding, the entrant would be unable to bring her unique contribution to mutual exchange in abbey life. The variety of gifts and personal heritages among community members allows not only an intense interchange within—but a multidimensional contemplative sharing with those who come to the abbey as guests, scholars and collaborators.

Appreciation of the masculine-feminine dimensions of human life is characteristic of the abbey. Men as well as women collaborate in the works of the abbey and this is particularly evident in the land programs. Through the years young men and women from various nations (students, foresters, surgeons, linguists, horticulturists) have come to work with beef and dairy herds, sheep and pigs, orchards and fields. The land becomes an integration point for them as they work, study and pray under the guidance of abbey members.

It is commonplace to speak of the earth as feminine. Theologically, this is important for the abbey and for the women and men who participate in caring for the land entrusted to the monastic community. Walter Bruggemann takes particular notice of the feminine quality of the earth in his essay, "Land: Fertility and Justice," noting the close parallels between the treatment of women and the utilization of land. Two temptations accompany woman-man relations, says Bruggemann: promiscuity and domination. The same temptations are rampant in the use of land:

> In our society we have terribly distorted relations between men and women.... We shall not have a new land ethic until we have a new sexual ethic, free of both promiscuity and domination. Applied to the land, we shall not have fertility until we have justice toward the land and toward those who depend on the land for life, which means all the brothers and sisters.[14]

In choosing what animals and crops should be raised on abbey land, as well as in deciding what kind of buildings will be erected, there is a sensitivity to the land within the context of human relationships. For that reason, the abbey sponsored a series of seminars for members and collaborators, dealing with both macro and micro aspects of earth. When world planner Buckminster Fuller came, he lectured for seven hours in the abbey's barn loft, the only gathering place at the time that could accommodate community and guests. Bales of hay served as chairs as Fuller expounded on the need for comprehensive vision and the conserving of earth's resources. The following day a geologist discussed the mysteries hidden in rocks and soil. He spoke movingly of breaking open a rock formed four million years ago: "I never get over it. It has never seen light of day since that time. I am privileged to dig in it–that breaks me up. I still cry about that."[15] One seminar was devoted to bees, and their interaction with other creatures–another year it was earthworms and their significance for life and earth. Such focused study provides insights that find their way not only into the care of farm and gardens, but also into prayer, spiritual direction, chant and art. Belden Lane observes:

> One never decides that "this" will be a sacred place–because of the beautiful view or the proximity to the village or the number of people who pass that way. "In actual fact, the place is never 'chosen' by man," says Eliade. "It is merely discovered by him; in other words, the sacred place in some way or another reveals itself to him".... Ultimately the holy exists entirely apart from any human control. It demands its own freedom to choose.[16]

The meaning of monastic enclosure is closely linked to recognition of "place" and land as holy. In a concerted dedication to praise God, to come into union within a given place, the contemplative is invited, *called* to bring into integration the multiple, incredibly unlimited aspects of creation within a given space, and to taste their blessedness. Such an understanding of monastic enclosure is akin to Raymond Ellis' "choosing one." Through loving "this" land and space, in all of its extensions, in relation to all who dwell on or visit it, there is the possibility of loving not only every creature, but the supreme giver of all, the creator.

Thus the Community of Regina Laudis places high priority on personal experience of the land in its woundedness and its potential. Soil and climate pose constant challenges. Stone walls in long grey ribbons grace the arching hills, but they also testify to the ritual described in Robert Frost's "Mending Wall." Winter moisture works between neatly piled stones, toppling them into fields; it also works beneath the soil, the ground frost propelling a new crop of stones to the surface each spring. There is struggle among all the members of the ecosystem: bringing land to fruitfulness means coping with rodents, insects, weeds–and weather in all its vagaries. Whenever possible, the abbey employs natural means to control enemies of crops and flowers.

Earth as Another "Book of Revelation"

Proper treatment of soil ultimately resides in a faith perspective. The earth is another book of Revelation, said a community member. "It is another Scripture, but to get to it, you have to live with it." She spoke of experiencing communion with the earth in terms of gravity, and realizing what torture it would be to remain vertical, upright at all times. Gravity draws one to the earth: to be horizontal is the position of relaxation and rest. So much is in "position" itself, she observed, "How hard it is to eat when one is lying down!" She, as many in the community, speaks, then, of a reciprocity, a mutual communing with earth. It is a communion and attentiveness that requires penance as well as joy. "There is a tremendous penance in learning submission to the earth because you are in control of nothing," the nun said. Familiarity with earth, receptivity to its gifts can also be a form of mutuality that is overwhelming. A warm, moist New England evening is sometimes followed by a cold winter night, producing thick hoarfrost on every branch:

> The sun comes up splendid, out of banks of cloud, shooting through the ice. The world becomes absolutely dazzling. It "hurts"–you can't stand it, you know. You think: if only we could hold this; you reflect how an artist paints a small canvas, marked "do not touch." Here, God does the whole world that way. By afternoon, God says, "Well, let's erase this and do another one!" Every weed, every little stone–the world is apocalyptic!

Each human body-person is a unique personification of earth, dust brought to consciousness, participating in the marvelous exchange of electrons, molecules and elements that at one moment are part of the soil beneath one's feet, next a delight to eye and palate, and then part of lip, brain or thigh. Exchange with the earth is evident. It is not surprising that exquisite hoarfrost laced on blue sky should dazzle the one who contemplates and almost exceed what one can bear. There is a fragile reciprocal relation between the human and the nonhuman. To reverence the dust from which human life emerges is to respond to Belden Lane's questions regarding "theology of place." He asks, "How can one develop a legitimate theology of place–being able to recognize once again the shekinah glory of a God we thought altogether driven from the world?... [I]s it possible to recover the power of sacred space for those today who have forgotten hierophanies and all signs of the sacred?"[17] Theology of place is not grounded in abstractions, but in dust, flowers and hoarfrost. St. Paul cautioned that humans do not "own" their bodies and John Hart warns that humans do not "own" the earth–that larger body from which they emerge, and to which they return:

> Because we are made in God's image and likeness, we have been given a special trust during our tenure on the land. We have been given charge of the earth and are God's vicarious owners–but only to the extent that we, like God, create what is good and work with the earth to meet the needs of the earth's creatures. We have been chosen to image God in our attitude toward, and practices upon, the earth. We are called to be God's stewards upon the land.[18]

The Benedictine patience in *living* the abbey into its milieu springs from an integral approach, from working with the land in trust, as God's vicarious owners. Loving, mutual presence to an "other" is always based in growing knowledge of that other. To learn the secrets of earth, even in an introductory manner within a given "place," takes time. Various tribes, along with multitudes of various species, inhabited the land long before it became an abbatial foundation. It is possible to "colonize" the land within a limited horizon and to act as if civilized dominion of the earth arrived with sacks of pesticide and the post-hole augur. Then occurs what Walter Bruggemann terms promiscuity and dominance rather than relationship with the land. Mutuality with the earth, respectful of gifts to be given and received, requires time: time to learn something of the ways that bees dance at the threshold of the hive to communicate the direction of clovers, each waiting with hundreds of brimming honey pots in their blossoms. It requires time to learn the location of hidden springs and the habits of raccoons.

The abbey community saws and stacks forest logs for winter warmth, and keeps a clarion chanticleer close to the abbey chapel. When a "place" is cared for within a loving wholeness, there is a sense of presence. Belden Lane says:

> [S]imply moving into an allegedly sacred place does not necessarily make one present to it.... This is a basic paradox of existence.... [O]ur being so often estranged from place means that we tragically are able to occupy the space without actually "dwelling" within it as place. Hence, even though we stand on the inaccessible ground of the holy, we may never yet have been brought into any relationship to it.[19]

The "place" of Regina Laudis is consciously developed within an integrated mutuality of soil, vegetative and animal life, and human toil. Wool from the sheep is spun, dyed with natural hues, shaped into vestments, garments and works of art. Shuttles slip through looms in the compact art studios over the milking barn. Meals for community and guests are predominantly prepared from foods provided by farm and gardens: cheeses and ice cream, vegetables, fruits and eggs, and fresh year-round greens from the "sun-pit." What has been reverently raised and prepared is then taken into the body as form of praise, as extension of eucharistic life.

Entrance Chapel: The Mystery of Eden

In 1984, the community added a new guest entrance to the original red-samba abbey building. The contemplative artist who received abbey guests had suggested that the community's growth required a new architectural idiom for the chapel entrance–one that would communicate a feminine spirit of lightsome joy, verdant fruitfulness and unexpected color. This would be especially helpful during the long winter months.

The entrance chapel now suggests the mystery of Eden "through the symbolic language of nature and art wedded in sacred space."[20] An entrance-cum-greenhouse, it abounds with flowers and plants, accenting the liturgical seasons. The entrance has become a garden enclosed where guests can be received within a sacramental aura. Over the door is a vibrant stained glass window of Our Lady and the Child, particularly luminous in the winter months.

Flowers and herbs are hallmarks of the abbey. The abbess, who has a particular gift for raising and arranging flowers, prepares the floral arrangements that grace the pinewood chapel where the hours of the divine office are chanted day and night. For Abbess Duss, flowers represent a very fragile aspect of glory: not a final glory, but an "indication" of the splendor of Christ. She sees profound meaning in the Chinese proverb: Only the rose is fragile enough to evoke eternity.

Following theological study of the sense of smell and the meaning of incense in liturgical worship, the community's herbologist worked with a specialist to select fourteen scents which are typical of abbey fields, gardens and chapel. These were combined to form "OSB Fragrance," available to guests after they had prayed and worked with the community. Of all the senses, the sense of smell is the most evocative of memories and past experience. Other fragrances have been prepared through the years, allowing guests to bear with them something of the work of their hands, something of the spiritual encounter they have known at the abbey. In order that they might know the full cycle of work and prayer in their bodies, each guest is invited to spend some time daily working on the land, bringing it to fruitfulness, struggling with stone, willful branch and weed.

Animal care is a demanding aspect of farm work: dairy and beef herds, sheep, pigs and chickens not only provide income and food (the community observes a meatless diet)–they are a vital point of interchange with guests and collaborators. Children who participate in the abbey's catechetical program are also able to know an appropriate relationship to animal life and care.[21] The land and its extensions literally become an active field of interchange with clergy and laity, and with professionals from various disciplines. At times, university departments of agriculture send students to the abbey to observe its approach to animal and land care.

One graphic form of collaboration between monastics and the larger community is the annual abbey fair which spills across guest lawns and abbey fields the first weekend of each August. It is a monastic tradition from the Middle Ages brought to contemporary expression, a joyful interface among monastery, neighbors and urban dwellers (in a recent year one hundred thousand people from the northeastern United States megalopolis shared the fair experience). Besides booths of clothing, wholesome foods, artistic creations, crafts and games, there is an annual major stage production in the outdoor theater: guest actors, musicians and dancers integrate members of associated lay communities and children from the abbey's catechetical program into these productions. The community tries, increment by increment, to bring the fair into deeper integration with the wholeness it strives for in daily life. The variety of talents and professional expertise among community members, and their ongoing development within contemplative life, prove significant for mutual work with farmers, film and stage artists, sculptors, medical doctors, lawyers, nurses, musicians, linguists, bakers, horticulturists, blacksmiths, bookbinders, beekeepers and potters (to name a cross-section).

The abbey, however, is not a place of escape from the corridor of waste products strewn along railroad tracks leading into New York City, nor is it a place for romantic nonactivity. These monastics can be likened to ice dancers, daily schooled in the discipline of practice, the ache of sore muscles and the move from one difficult leap to the next.[22] Guests enter into that world of prayerful challenge. Their struggle to discern and deepen personal vocation ever more clearly is worked out in relation to wood chipper and bailer in the fields, as well as in the chapel. Abbess and community always speak in terms of ever-deepening efforts rather than *accomplished* integration. Members who come with accomplished gifts in one area of life are not instantly aware of all the dimensions of contemplative integration among prayer, community life, earth and profession. It is a lifelong process of mutually integrating the various levels. There is a constant learning from creation itself, a learning that frequently comes only through struggle and suffering. The rhythm of animal life and death signs this.

Of Animals, Sacrifice, and the Flesh of Christ

Although the community maintains a meatless diet, it raises animals for guests and for those who purchase abbey meats which are free from contamination. The accidental death of an animal is especially painful. One who cares for the herds spoke of finding a cow that had died after being caught in a wooden partition. She observed that when animals sense imminent death, their eyes are fixed in terror: it is indeed a finality. There is, however, a mutuality between human and animals when they are received as human nourishment, she noted. Although there is a goodness in the natural life and death of animals, there is often a terrible finality in it. But for an animal taken as human food, the life and death cycle of the animal (or fowl or fish) enters into human consciousness and the human capacity to choose, to praise, to pray. That which would have plateaued with animal death can now participate in the lived body that brings conscious praise of God, as limited as that participation is.

There is an incomparable dignity in human, bodied life. It is a microcosm of the universe, incorporating soil, vegetative and animal life into relationship with the triune God. There is a marvelous mutual exchange in this: having been poured out in self-gift, fruits and animals of the earth receive the gift of participation in conscious relational life. In this mutuality with the earth, chicken and pig, lamb and cow lose life, but *through* humans are released into another level of expression: into contemplative chant, into closer relation with the divine/human Lamb who was slain. The Second Reading, Friday, Fifth Week of Lent, has it:

> The sacrifices of animal victims which our forefathers were commanded to offer to God by the Holy Trinity itself, the one God of the old and the new testaments, foreshadowed the most acceptable gift of all. This was the offering which

> in his compassion the only Son of God would make of himself in his human nature for our sake.... In the time of the Old Testament, patriarchs, prophets and priests sacrificed animals in his honor, and in honor of the Father and the Holy Spirit as well....Those animal sacrifices foreshadowed the flesh of Christ which he would offer for our sins, though himself without sin, and the blood which he would pour out for the forgiveness of our sins.[23]

It is not surprising that Christmas tales, fashioned in various cultures through the centuries, abound with speaking animals whose presence at the crèche brings nourishment, warmth and song. Luke's explicit mention of Christ's being placed in a manger invites such playful insights. What Henry David Thoreau and Annie Dillard perceived can serve as entrance point for an incarnational contemplative understanding of creation. Not by traversing the breadth of the earth, but by opening themselves to the mystery of a very finite place did they come to know and love the earth–it was Tinker Creek for Dillard; Walden Pond for Thoreau. The abbey is such a "place" of depth interchange. What children intimate in their first naivete is a promise, a glimpse of conscious mutuality with all creation. As philosopher Paul Ricoeur pointed out, the mere shattering of first naivete through experience is not the fullness of becoming or the attainment of wisdom. It is the possibility for a second naivete, chastened by suffering. In asking whether or not it is possible to recover the power of sacred space today, Belden Lane appeals to Ricoeur's insight concerning the hermeneutical circle

> by which one moves from an original naivete, with its easy immediacy of belief, through a necessary process of criticism and demythologization to a "second-naivete" by which wonder is restored, chastened of its earlier confusion and credulity. [Ricoeur] insists that "the dissolution of the myth as explanation is the necessary way to the restoration of the myth as symbol. This is the recovery of myth in all its power and awe, while retaining the insistent demands of intellectual objectivity".... Places *can* be formative of our very being as humans, rooting us at the deepest levels of mystery and meaning.[24]

Wonder is chastened of confusion and credulity when incessant rains pound new-mown hay into the stubble, or a perfectly-formed lamb lies upon the shelter floor, awaiting burial. Reality trickles down the back with aching immediacy at August baling time; it works its way beneath fingernails at the carrot harvest. The convergence of wonder, struggle, and transcendent faith comes in the mystery of the incarnation, which has marked the Regina Laudis foundation from its inception.

The Abbey of Regina Laudis serves as an example of mutuality with the earth through its land program only because program activities are part of a larger sense of mutuality and interchange rooted in the incarnation and the eucharist. It is significant, then, that community members work in "triads" as they carry forward specific projects, and that the entrance chapel welcomes guests with a small trinitarian fountain, sign of the abbey's union with other religious communities. Regina Laudis is a sacred "place" where earth groans, flowers, comes to fruition in sacramental repetition.

CHAPTER SEVEN

That They May Be One as We Are One

> Jesus says, "The glory which Thou hast given me I have given to them, that they may be one, even as we are one, I in them, Thou in me" (Jn 17:22–3). In this present experience of mutual indwelling, the depths of which are attested to by the saints and mystics, we can get a present foreshadowing of what Paul means when he says that the goal of creation is the mutual indwelling of God and the creation, in which God will be all in all. *–John J. O'Donnell*[1]

Jesus Christ, the embodied revelation of divine mutual indwelling, brought into the commonalities of daily life the possibility of human participation in divine perichoresis. Hans Urs von Balthasar observed that it might *seem* a better thing to abandon attempts at thinking and speaking about God who, even through revelation remains so wholly "other." "But," he says, "we no longer have authority to do this, for he came to us in an event–which had its climax in Christ Jesus–of such self-giving, defenseless, inviting power...that we understand at least so much: he wants to be *for us,* he wants to gather us into the abyss of his own inner trinitarian love."[2] Jesus' incarnated revelation came through simple words and gestures: he came as theology in the flesh and spoke in the images of fruitful vines, dwelling places, food and drink. Without the fleshly arch of the incarnation, joining divine perichoretic love with human life, any thought of intimate divine-human mutuality would have remained an abstraction, a remote ideal.

At the last supper, Jesus prayed "that they may be one as we are one. With me in them and you in me" (Jn 17:22–23). He was not merely suggesting this by way of eschatological fulfillment, but as *a way of being* meant to characterize earthly existence, beginning with those gathered at the supper. That is why it has been necessary to probe the meaning of mutuality within the context of bodily existence, and the concrete realities of daily life. Jesus' prayer for mutual indwelling followed an act so bodily (seemingly so unworthy of him) that it embarrassed the fisherman, Peter: the washing of feet. It was following that simple act that Jesus inextricably bonded the receiving and ingestion of food and drink with his own total self-gift. This bodiliness–this intimacy of divine and human within the most earthy of human needs–remains scandalous for some, even after millennia of Christian experience and reflection. Yet, it was precisely within this context that Jesus offered his revelatory prayer and teaching regarding the disciples' relationships with him, the Father and the Holy Spirit (to the extent that they could receive it before the coming of the Holy Spirit, who would bring to their minds all that had been given to them). In the final hours before he handed himself over into a death that would make his self-gift accessible to people of all ages, Jesus offered his disciples a participation in the inner life of God (a reality that had seemed so remote from their ordinary life tasks).

The Enduring Meaning of Christ's Sacred Humanity

In the "Sixth Mansion" of *The Interior Castle,* Teresa of Avila described a variety of mystical gifts, and then commented, "It will also seem to you that anyone who enjoys such lofty things will no longer meditate on the mysteries of the most sacred humanity of our Lord Jesus Christ."[3] She refutes such an attitude by reminding her readers that withdrawal from corporeal things is not characteristic of those who are expressed in the body, but of angelic spirits. For one in the "Seventh Mansion" there is union with the Trinity: "[A]ll three Persons communicate themselves to it, speak to it, and explain those words of the Lord in the Gospel: that He and the Father and the Holy Spirit will come to dwell with the soul that loves Him and keeps His commandments."[4] It is significant that Teresa links her *experience* of divine indwelling with the dailiness of life:

> [T]hese Persons never seem to leave it anymore.... In the extreme interior, in some place very deep within itself, the nature of which it doesn't know how to explain...it perceives this divine company. You may think that as a result

> the soul will be outside itself and so absorbed that it will be unable to be occupied with anything else. On the contrary, the soul is much more occupied than before with everything pertaining to the service of God; and once its duties are over it remains with that enjoyable company.[5]

For the purposes of this reflection on mutuality, it is not Teresa's extraordinary mystical gifts of divine interpenetrating presence that need emphasis: it is her counsel that the deepest union with the Trinity leads to increased self-gift in very earthy ways. Her personal accounts of "The Foundations" and her letters are eloquent in this regard. Her experience of mutuality with divine life is punctuated by the running of the bulls in dark Spanish towns, of sewage raining down from upper windows, of crude inn-dwellers, lizards and pounding noises in the head! Teresa's insights accord with gospel accounts. Jesus, according to Matthew, invited his followers to consider the lilies, sparrows–even the hair on their heads–to gain some inkling of God's providential nearness. Following the intensity of revelation at the last supper, the gospels record, there was a cool walk into the Valley of Cedron, exhaustion, sleep, terror, flailing swords, a betraying kiss, and denials laced with expletives. Neither the gospels nor Teresa are sentimental regarding mutual love, mutual indwelling.

The mystery of mutuality includes multiple paradoxes, seeming contradictions that can scandalize at times, cause some to lose the stomach for seeking it–or, that can prove the entry point for the possibility of reciprocal self-gift and mutual indwelling opened by Jesus in his revelation of divine life. That revelation was as immediate as spittled clay rubbed into blind eyes, or post-resurrection breakfast around a charcoal fire. The theology of mutuality will always be a theology of the body and the blood, given and received. It is a "*Donum* theology" or a theology of gift.

This study has been done from the perspective of Catholic faith that acknowledges all creation as sacramental and professes belief in the intense presence of divine life within creation. Such a perspective is valid only when uniqueness and distinction are reverenced within the union. John Hart says:

> God has created us; the earth gives us life. We are, then, children of God and children of Mother Earth. We are part

> of that totality of creation that emanated from God; we are part of that community of relation that is rooted in the earth. Yet, we are unique in both cases. Although part of creation, we are the only part made in God's image and likeness and the only part appointed to be co-creators and trustees of the earth. Although part of the integrated community that is the earth, we are, as is every part, genetically distinct and having our own physical and social needs and species destiny. Our religious dimension adds another aspect of uniqueness to us: we are the only part of the physical creation that is conscious of being created by God and that can acknowledge its gratitude to and love for God.[6]

In genuine mutuality, identity and distinction must be respected or there cannot be authentic union. Even when each being is encountered as an esteemed "other," there must be vigilance in a wounded world, lest domination and sheer "utilization" displace appropriate, life-enhancing interchange.

It is the task of theologians to make distinctions, to formulate theories, and to choose adequate language regarding an ordered body of knowledge about God, about the divine plan for the universe, and about the multiple interrelationships flowing from that saving plan. Today, however, there is a serious crisis within the theological community: disagreements are rife concerning the methods, content, purpose and authority of theology—as well as its relation to faith and practical religious living. While serious disagreements have always accompanied theological endeavors, there is a new intensity and breadth to these disagreements, often making fruitful dialogue difficult or impossible. Crises have positive as well as negative elements: they often signal what I have referred to earlier as "fullness of time" for renewed insight. The current crisis in theology has stirred creative advances—among them, a vigorous attempt to lay theological foundations for a spirituality of interpersonal relationships. The crisis has also underscored the need for theologians to clarify the context and purpose of their work.

Conscious decisions were made in carrying out the research and writing of the present book: 1) to reverence the dogmatic tradition received within the Roman Catholic tradition, seeing each basic belief not as outmoded, but rather as an aspect of a totality received as revelatory gift (which at times may seem incongruous, but having unhorizoned possibility, and always exceeding human calculation); 2) to bring theological theory into relation with embodied life; and 3) to integrate insights from related disciplines and life experience when these contribute to an understanding of mutuality rooted in trinitarian theology.

Mutuality, in its multiple levels and forms of expression, has its source in divine inner communion. Mutuality refers, first of all, to *perichoresis,* or *circuminsessio,* that mutual indwelling of divine persons, forever totally given in reciprocal self-gift, that is constitutive of divine life. That is why George Maloney says of the human vocation to perichoretic self-gift: "We are this way because God is this way in his essence as Love." All of creation bears some vestige of divine mutuality, no matter how this is appropriately expressed among the myriads of creatures.

In light of the divine paradigm, I have suggested that the fundamental category of being or existence is not substance or process, but *gift, a category transcending all philosophical systems and categories.* The total self-gift among divine persons, and its imaging in human life, form the basis of all human discourse and interaction. The entire universe participates in reciprocal giving and receiving, since it is made according to the pattern of the creator. From a faith perspective, the world is sacramental, signing with extravagant diversity the most fundamental reality: *self-gift* (from subatomic particles, through the water cycle, to conscious, personal, human self-gift). Where there is integral self-gift, it will not be swallowed up within a one-on-one relationship, but will be fruitful in countless "thirds." If integrity is lacking within symbolic reality (dishonest placing of body into act; withholding of gift; domination; and the excluding or controlling of the other), relationships erode, and interchange becomes violent, even deadly. Such human confrontations extend into the environment, causing cataclysmic devastation, even though such devastation may remain imperceptible or seem minor over a period of time.

Jesus Christ is the bonding point, the enduring expression of total self-gift, the embodied realization of divine-human giving and receiving. In his visible earthly life Jesus consistently brought persons and things into fruitful relationship: soil-seed-sower-kingdom; net-fish-fisher-apostle; leaven-bread-bakerwoman-eucharist. He opened his followers to the unguessed potential for synergistic union within the simplest of earthly beings and actions. To be human is to be called to perichoretic self-gift, in and through the body. As Jesus knew and experienced, this means a willingness to suffer the forgetfulness, selfishness, treachery and betrayal of others.

Mutuality: The Ultimate Leap of Trust

There is particular delight in those art forms which require deliberate trust and risk in relationship: for example, ice dancing, pairs figure skating, and trapeze artistry. In these art forms, total attentiveness toward the other is required, a trust that allows gravity-defying leaps. In trapeze-trampoline ballet, performers must "let go" across chasms, trusting that they will be met by welcoming arms suspended from a fragile trapeze. There is constant interchange, a going out toward the others in trust. It is one level of mutuality in visual, embodied art. It is not surprising that divine-human interchange is sometimes referred to as a dance, or that the incarnation is described as the almighty Word leaping down from heaven. In Luke's account of the visitation there is an inner-outer dance and interchange. Mary's greeting sounded in Elizabeth's ears; John leapt to greet the Christ in Mary's womb; Elizabeth received revelation in and through her own body and the bodies of those coming into union; and Mary burst into a song of praise. It was an encounter of four, caught up in trinitarian mutuality. It was a perichoretic exchange, at once celibate and nuptial, in Cyril's terms "a real, physical union." Openness to mutuality can open fresh avenues of communion among laity, priests and religious; it can also awaken new appreciation for the largely untapped potential for interchange among the members of the communion of saints. As B. R. Brinkman pointed out in his explication of consummative intimacy, the sacramental community of faith has much to learn from the "cognate" forms of intimacy regarding its own intimate communion. To receive these insights, it is essential that the people of God delve deeply into what has been given within the wholeness of trinitarian faith. Robert Brungs says:

> If I were to make just one recommendation for the future...it would be this: remember, we live in God and God lives in us. It is our duty to translate this union into

the sacramental development of the final Kingdom of God, which will embrace all of created reality. Rarely has any generation been blessed with such a challenge. We must become reacquainted with the riches of the Christian tradition about the unity of all things in Christ.[7]

Notes

Preface

[1] Sister Maura Eichner, SSND, "Notes for an Autobiography," in *What We Women Know* (West Lafayette, IN, 1980), p. 34.

Chapter One

[1] Richard of St. Victor, "Book Three of the Trinity," in *Richard of St. Victor,* trans. and introd. Grover A. Zinn, Classics of Western Spirituality series (Toronto, 1979), p. 384. Unless otherwise indicated, subsequent quotations from Richard's text are from this translation.

[2] Cf. Jn 16:12. Unless attributed to other sources, all scriptural translations are from *The Jerusalem Bible,* ed. Alexander Jones, et al. (Garden City, NY, 1966).

[3] See Ewert Cousins, "A Theology of Interpersonal Relations," *Thought,* XLV, 176 (Spring 1970), p. 58.

[4] Cousins, p. 82.

[5] Donald L. Gelpi, *The Divine Mother: A Trinitarian Theology of the Holy Spirit* (Washington, DC, 1984), p.138.

[6] Leonardo Boff, *Trinity and Society* (Maryknoll, NY, 1988), pp. 118–119. Boff cites F. Tamans d'Eypernon, *Le mystère primordial: La Trinité sa vivante image* (Paris, 1950), esp. pp. 56–62; and Grom and Guerrero, *El anuncio,* pp. 36, 99–106.

[7] *Webster's Third International Dictionary,* ed. Philip Babcock Gove and staff (Springfield, MA, 1981), p. 1493.

[8] Peter Henrici, "Modernity and Christianity," *Communio,* XVII, 2 (Summer 1990), pp. 146–147.

[9] Steve Mertl, "Personal computer conduit for ultimate in safe

sex," in *The Star Phoenix* (June 13, 1992), Saskatoon, Saskatchewan, p. E8.

[10] Kenneth Schmitz, "Postmodern or modern-plus?" *Communio,* XVII, 2 (Summer 1990), p. 158.

[11] Schmitz, p. 161.

[12] Dorothee Soelle, "Thou Shalt Have No Other Jeans Before Me," in *The Challenge of Liberation Theology: A First World Response,* ed. Brian Mahan and L. Dale Richesin (Maryknoll, NY, 1981), pp. 8–9.

[13] Cited by Priscilla Painton and Elizabeth Taylor in "Love and Let Die," *Time,* 136, 12 (19 March 1990), p. 56.

[14] James Gleick, *Chaos: Making a New Science* (New York, 1987), p. 8.

[15] Gleick, p. 23.

[16] James B. Irwin, with William A. Emerson, Jr., *To Rule the Night* (Nashville, TN, 1982), p. 17.

[17] Irwin, p. 17.

[18] See Pope John Paul II, *Original Unity of Man and Woman* (Boston, MA, 1981) and subsequent edited collections of audiences from the same publisher: *Blessed are the Pure of Heart* (1983); *Reflections on Humanae Vitae* (1984); and *The Theology of Marriage and Celibacy* (1986).

[19] See Walter Ong, *Fighting for Life* (London, 1981), p. 208.

Chapter Two

[1] Pope John Paul II, *On the Holy Spirit in the Life of the Church and the World,* issued 1986, Vatican trans. (Boston, MA, n.d.), #10, p. 18.

[2] Church Fathers saw indications of the Trinity in Gen. 1:26: "God said, 'Let us make man in our own image, in the likeness of ourselves,'" but there is no indication that the Priestly redactor intended such an interpretation.

[3] See Royce Gordon Gruenler, *The Trinity in the Gospel of John: A Thematic Commentary on the Fourth Gospel* (Grand Rapids, MI, 1986), p. 5.

[4] John Paul II, *Holy Spirit,* #9, p. 17.

[5] "He will glorify me,/since all he tells you/will be taken from what is mine./Everything the Father has is mine;/that is why I said:/All he tells you/will be taken from what is mine."

[6] Gruenler, p. 117.

[7] Raymond E. Brown, *The Gospel According to John I–XII,* Anchor Bible, Vol. 29 (Garden City, NY, 1966), pp. 511–512.

[8] Raymond E. Brown, *The Gospel According to John XIII–XXI*, Anchor Bible, Vol. 29A (Garden City, NY, 1970), p. 639.

[9] Brown, *John XIII–XXI*, p. 642.

[10] See Gruenler, p. xvii.

[11] From author's personal notes: lecture on "Heidegger, Camus, and the film *Jules et Jim*," given by Rev. Arthur Gibson, University of St. Michael's College, University of Toronto, winter term, 1974.

[12] See Gibson lecture notes.

[13] Pope John Paul II, "Apostolic Letter on Augustine of Hippo," Vatican trans., *Origins*, 16, 16 (2 October 1986), p. 270.

[14] St. Augustine, *The Trinity*, trans. Stephen McKenna (Washington, DC, 1963). All subsequent references to Augustine's *The Trinity* are from this translation.

[15] Edmund Fortman, *The Triune God: A Historical Study of the Doctrine of the Trinity* (Grand Rapids, MI, 1972), p.144.

[16] See Richard of St. Victor, note* on p. 389.

[17] See Cousins, "A Theology of Interpersonal Relations," p. 62. Cousins links Richard's analysis with the total Christian experience:

> Behind Richard's analysis of interpersonal relations are centuries of Christian experience, in which the Christian community sought to live out the ideal of Christian charity in the light of faith. In meditating on its faith-transformed experience, the Christian community has grown in consciousness of its ideal of self-transcending love. Since Richard is heir to this long history of experience, he does not stand in a type of antiseptic chamber where rational categories are shielded from any contact with life. Nor does his experience itself exist in an historical vacuum, apart from the transforming power of centuries of Christian faith (pp. 62–63).

[18] Cousins, p. 69.

[19] See John J. O'Donnell, *Trinity and Temporality: The Christian Doctrine of God in the Light of Process Theology and the Theology of Hope* (Oxford University Press, 1983), p. 54, commenting on Moltmann's *The Crucified God*, pp. 255–256.

[20] See James D. Spiceland, "Process Theology," in *One God in Trinity*, ed. Peter Toon and James D. Spiceland (Westchester, IL, 1980), p. 136.

[21] See Spiceland, p. 136.

[22] Spiceland, p. 136.

[23] See O'Donnell, *Trinity and Temporality*, p. 74, for a discussion of Whitehead's God-concept as presented in A. N. Whitehead, *Process and Reality: An Essay in Cosmology* (New York, 1929).

[24] Joseph A. Bracken, *The Triune Symbol: Persons, Process and Community* (New York, 1985), p. 5.

[25] Bracken, p. 44.

[26] Bracken, p. 44.

[27] Bracken, p. 43.

[28] William Hill, *The Three-Personed God: The Trinity as Mystery of Salvation* (Washington, DC, 1982), p. 210.

[29] Bracken, p. 51.

[30] Bracken, p. 20.

[31] See Anthony Kelly, "Trinity and Process: Relevance of the Basic Christian Confession of God," *Theological Studies,* 31, 3 (1970), pp. 395–396.

[32] See Bruno Forte, *l'Eglise icône de la Trinité* (Paris, 1985), p. 12.

[33] "Decree for the Jacobites," Council of Florence, 1442, trans. in *The Teaching of the Catholic Church,* ed. Karl Rahner (Staten Island, NY, 1967), p. 100.

[34] Boff, pp. 135–136.

[35] See A. M. Bermejo, "Circumincession," *New Catholic Encyclopedia,* Vol. III (San Francisco, 1967), p. 880.

[36] See Brian Hebblethwaite, "Perichoresis–Reflections on the Doctrine of the Trinity," *Theology,* LXXX, 676 (July 1977), pp. 255–261.

[37] See E. Louis Backman, *Religious Dances in the Christian Church and in Popular Medicine,* trans. E. Classen (Westport, CT, reprinted 1977), p. 27.

[38] "Trinity of the Old Testament," *The Feasts of Rus: Icon Calendar Book* (Toronto, 1991), n.p.

[39] Hebblethwaite, pp. 255–256.

[40] Richard Schneider, "The Human Person as the Image of the Three-Personal God," lecture, Marquette University, Milwaukee, Wisconsin, August 8, 1966, pp. 1–2.

[41] Schneider, pp. 8–9.

[42] Karl Rahner and Herbert Vorgrimler, *Theological Dictionary,* ed. Cornelius Ernst, trans. Richard Strachan (New York, 1965), p. 471.

[43] John Paul II, *Holy Spirit,* p. 18.

[44] John Paul II, *Holy Spirit*, p. 18.
[45] O'Donnell, *Triune God*, p. 140.

Chapter Three

[1] George A. Maloney, "A Trinitarian Church of One in Many: A Mysticism of Community," *Diakonia*, XV, 1 (1980), p. 201.
[2] Martin Buber, *I and Thou*, trans. Walter Kaufmann (New York, 1970), p. 54. Unless otherwise indicated, subsequent citations are from this translation.
[3] Buber, p. 55.
[4] Buber, p. 56.
[5] Buber, p. 59.
[6] Donald L. Berry, *Mutuality: The Vision of Martin Buber* (Albany, NY, 1985), p. 34.
[7] See Anton C. Pegis, "The Notion of Man in the Context of Renewal," in *Theology of Renewal*, ed. L. K. Shook (New York, 1968), I, p. 264; and Berry, *Mutuality*, pp. 29–30.
[8] Buber, p. 178.
[9] Buber, p. 172.
[10] Buber, p. 173.
[11] Buber, p. 173.
[12] Buber, p. 174.
[13] Buber, p. 155.
[14] Buber, p. 158.
[15] Buber, p. 158.
[16] Buber, p. 182.
[17] Buber, p. 78.
[18] See Jean-Paul Sartre, *Being and Nothingness: An Essay on Phenomenological Ontology*, trans. Hazel E. Barnes (New York, 1956), p. 290.
[19] Sartre, p. 259.
[20] Sartre, p. 338.
[21] See Harriet Goldhor Lerner, *The Dance of Intimacy* (New York, 1989), pp. 143–161.
[22] Aaron O. Wassermann, *Biology* (New York, 1973), p. .20.
[23] David H. Freedman, "Weird Science," *Discover*, XI, 11 (November 1990), p. 62.
[24] Irwin, p. 19.
[25] Irwin, pp. 18, 22.

[26] See also Maloney, p. 211.

[27] Karl Rahner, "On the Theology of the Incarnation," in *Theological Investigations* IV, trans. Kevin Smyth (Baltimore, MD, 1966), p. 108.

[28] Douglas V. Steere attributes this saying to Kollwitz in *Mutual Irradiation: A Quaker View of Ecumenism* (Pendle Hill Pamphlet 175, n.d.), p. 6.

[29] Hans Urs von Balthasar, "Christian Prayer," *Communio*, V, 1 (Spring 1978), p. 21.

[30] Edward Schillebeeckx, *Christ the Sacrament of the Encounter with God* (New York, 1963), p. 14.

[31] See "Dogmatic Constitution on the Church," in *The Documents of Vatican II,* ed. Walter M. Abbott, trans. ed. Joseph Gallagher (New York, 1966), #1, p. 15.

[32] See Nathan R. Wood, *The Trinity in the Universe* (Grand Rapids, MI, 1978), p. 105.

[33] Schillebeeckx, p. 15.

[34] A recent example of bringing incongruity to a mirthful resolution occurred shortly before the Berlin Wall was demolished. The international congregation of the School Sisters of Notre Dame had members on either side of the Wall. The Berlin Provincial Superior, having received the gift of a sculpted image of the community's foundress, Blessed Theresa of Jesus Gerhardinger, had taken it to East Berlin where it was blessed. At the border, on her return to the west, there was a difficulty, described in a letter to the SSND community:

> The guards...would not let Mother Theresa cross the border, because "she did not have a visa," as they said. For about four hours Sister Beata was questioned by three different people and explained over and over again that the statue was not Our Lady or an antique piece of art, but our foundress, recently carved and now given as a present to the Sisters in West Berlin. All was in vain. They would not allow her to take Mother Theresa home from the check-point Sonnenllee to our mission in Neukolln, only five minutes away. After several weekly visits at the border Sister Beata reported there again on June 13. When they again refused her request, she said that on June 20 all the sisters would come in procession with candles and flowers to congratulate Mother Theresa on

her birthday. The prospect brought a change. On June 17 Mother Theresa was allowed to enter West Berlin. (Letter, SSND Generalate, Rome, 24 November 1990, p. 7)

[35] Christopher Fry, "The Lady's Not for Burning," in *Christopher Fry Plays* (London, 1973), p. 165.

[36] Karl Rahner, "The Theology of the Symbol," in *Theological Investigations IV,* trans. Kevin Smyth (Baltimore, 1966), pp. 242–243.

[37] Rahner, "The Theology of the Symbol," p. 222.

[38] Rahner, "The Theology of the Symbol," p. 231.

[39] Rahner, "The Theology of the Symbol," p. 237.

[40] Rahner, "The Theology of the Symbol," p. 249.

[41] Arthur A. Vogel, *Body Theology: God's Presence in Man's World* (New York, 1973), p. 92.

[42] Vogel, p. 97.

[43] John Paul II, *Original Unity,* p. 109.

[44] John Paul II, *Original Unity*, p. 74.

[45] John Paul II, *Original Unity,* p. 102.

[46] John Paul II, *Original Unity,* p. 119.

[47] Robert A. Brungs, *You See Lights Breaking Upon Us: Doctrinal Perspectives on Biological Advance* (St. Louis, MO, 1989), p. 2. Brungs adds: "This urgent task is made more difficult because so few members of the Christian community understand its depth. There is an issue of greatest magnitude here, and the silence is appalling" (p. 2).

[48] Richard M. Zaner, *The Context of Self: A Phenomenological Inquiry Using Medicine as a Clue* (Athens, OH, 1981), p. 53.

[49] John Paul II, *Pure of Heart,* p. 258.

[50] Portions of student essays are quoted anonymously with permission of the writers.

[51] Rémi Brague, "On the Christian Model of Unity: The Trinity," *Communio,* X, 2 (Summer 1983), p. 161.

[52] John Paul II, *Original Unity,* p. 133.

Chapter Four

[1] Pope John Paul II, *Vocation and Mission of the Lay Faithful,* Vatican trans. (Sherbrooke, Que., 1989), pp. 43–44.

[2] See Phyllis Trible, *God and the Rhetoric of Sexuality* (Philadelphia, 1978), p. 33.

[3] Trible, p. 35.

[4] Trible, p. 38.

[5] Pope John Paul II, *On the Mercy of God,* issued 1980, Vatican trans. (Boston, MA, n.d.), p. 7.

[6] See John Paul II, *Mercy,* p. 42.

[7] John Paul II, *Mercy,* p. 42.

[8] See John Paul II, *Mercy,* p. 44.

[9] John Paul II, *Vocation and Mission,* pp. 101–102.

[10] See "Dogmatic Constitution on the Church," #10, p. 27.

[11] Pope John Paul II, *The Redeemer of Man,* issued 1979, Vatican trans. (Boston, MA, n.d.), p. 50.

[12] Pope John Paul II, "Holy Thursday Letter to Priests," Vatican trans. *Origins,* 18, 43 (6 April 1989), p. 731.

[13] See "Holy Spirit" in *Harper's Bible Dictionary,* ed. Paul J. Achtemeier (San Francisco, 1985), p. 401.

[14] Rahner and Vorgrimler, *Dictionary,* p. 211.

[15] See Acts 10.

[16] Pope Paul VI, *On the Renewal of the Religious Life According to the Teaching of the Second Vatican Council* (Boston, MA, 1971), p. 5.

[17] Paul VI, *Renewal,* p. 12.

[18] Maloney, p. 203.

[19] Maloney, p. 211.

[20] See B. R. Brinkman, "On Sacramental Man: II," *The Heythrop Journal,* XIV, 1 (January, 1973), p. 20.

[21] Brinkman, pp. 18–19.

[22] Brinkman, p. 11.

[23] Brinkman, p. 22.

[24] Brinkman, p. 23.

[25] Brown, *John I–XII,* pp. 284–285.

[26] Benedict M. Ashley, *Theologies of the Body: Humanist and Christian* (Braintree, MA, 1985), p. 663.

[27] Ashley, p. 664.

[28] Robert T. Sears, "Trinitarian Love as Ground of the Church," *Theological Studies,* 37 (December, 1976), p. 676.

[29] Maloney, p. 217.

[30] See Boff, p. 107.

[31] See Sears, pp. 668ff.

[32] See Sears, p. 667.

[33] See John W. de Crouchy quoted in "Heard at the Conference," *Catholic International,* 2, 2 (16–31 January 1991), p. 93.

[34] Sharon D. Welch, *Communities of Resistance and Solidarity: A Feminist Theology of Liberation* (Maryknoll, NY, 1985), p. 25.

[35] See John Paul II, *Pure of Heart*, pp. 257–258.

[36] See Brungs, *You See Lights*, p. 141.

[37] Brungs, *You See Lights*, pp. 147–148.

[38] See John Langan "Models and Values: The Search for U.S. Christian Community," in *Tracing the Spirit: Communities, Social Action, and Theological Reflection*, ed. James E. Hug (New York, 1983), p. 152; see also James W. Jones, "The Lure of Fellowship," *Cross Currents*, XXV, 1 (Winter 1977), pp. 422–423.

[39] Cardinal Joseph Ratzinger, in a personal interview with the author, The Holy Office, Rome (24 October 1990). He added that

> in living my fundamental vocation in love toward the other, I find God and I begin to know what *is* God, and to see God. So, I think there is an interdependency between the two relations...they are finally one relation. So, spiritual life in contact with God creates love toward the other, and realized love toward the other creates understanding of God, and creates spiritual life. I think this interdependence is very important.

[40] Paola Piscitelli, in a personal interview with the author, St. Egidio Language School, Trestevere, Rome, October 19, 1990.

[41] Piscitelli interview.

[42] The community has a Managing Council, periodically elected by a Plenary Assembly. Currently, the President is Professor Andrea Riccardi, one of the founding members of the Community of St. Egidio.

[43] The language school had approximately 3,000 registrants in 1989. Adults who have recently arrived in Italy learn Italian and English in order to gain employment and to enter into Italian society.

[44] See "The Community of St. Egidio" (Piazza S. Egidio, 3/a - 00153 Roma, Italia), p. 4.

[45] "St. Egidio: What is it?" information bulletin, n.d., p. 1.

[46] "Being with the Poor," in *Letters from S. Egidio*, Community Newsletter (February 1989), pp. 6–7.

[47] *Letters from S. Egidio*, p. 1.

[48] John Paul II, *Lay Faithful*, #20, p. 47.

[49] Individual names are not given from interviews with couples and

the entire community. These interviews were conducted during the summer, 1987.

[50] Each community has a unique origin and mission. At times the Sponsor Couples directly assist in the founding of these communities, or collaborate in their specific projects. A sense of call and mission has brought the following to form lay communities: medical doctors, infertile couples, lawyers, previously addicted youths, nurses, and professionals who serve the dying.

[51] Charles A. Gallagher, George A. Maloney, Mary F. Rousseau and Paul F. Wilczak, *Embodied in Love: Sacramental Spirituality and Sexual Intimacy* (New York, 1983), p. 119. The authors say of the church:

> Let us now look at the Church in a matrimonial context, as the Bride of Christ. For she is meant to be an even more basic symbolic realization of trinitarian love than are her sacramental married couples. Thus her visible fact–the visible, tangible, audible structures of the Church that people meet in their experience of her–ought to be an incarnation of love that is generous, tender and passionate (pp. 120–121).

[52] Gallagher, Maloney, Rousseau, and Wilczak, *Embodied in Love,* p. 119.

[53] Wendy M. Wright, "Reflections on Spiritual Friendship Between Men and Women," *Weavings* (Nashville, TN, n.d.), p. 18. (Personal copy of W. M. Wright). See also Wright, *Bond of Perfection: Jeanne de Chantal & François de Sales* (New York, 1985); and Bernadette Kimmerling, "Marriage, Friendship and Community," *The Furrow,* 31, 6 (June 1980), pp. 366–373.

Chapter Five

[1] Father Raymond Ellis, Pastor, St. Cecilia Parish, Detroit, MI, address to priests and religious educators of the Winona, Minnesota Diocese, February 22, 1971.

[2] John Paul II, *Lay Faithful,* #26, p. 62.

[3] John Paul II, *Lay Faithful,* #8, p. 24.

[4] John Paul II, *Lay Faithful,* #26, p. 62.

[5] John Paul II, *Lay Faithful,* #26, p. 62.

[6] Raymond Ellis, *The St. Cecilia Weekly* (July 4, 1965), p. 1.

[7] See Joseph Fox, "Toward a Theology of the Parish," Dissertation, Dominican House of Studies, Washington, DC, n.d., Appendix V, for detailed inner city analysis/plans, prepared in collaboration with the parish by three post-graduate students from the University of Detroit, as proposed by Francis A. Prokes, SJ, School of Architecture, and directed by Dean Bruno Leon.

[8] Ellis, *The Beacon* (April 21, 1968), p. 6.

[9] Ellis, Minnesota address.

[10] Ellis, Minnesota address.

[11] See Ellis, Minnesota address.

[12] Personal interview with DeVon Cunningham, Edison Center, Detroit, MI, July 21, 1987.

[13] Ellis, *The Beacon* (July 13, 1969), p. 4.

[14] Ellis, *The Beacon* (April 14, 1968), pp. 1, 6.

[15] Ellis, Minnesota address.

[16] Ellis, *The Beacon* (April 21, 1968), p. 6.

[17] Ellis, *The Beacon* (January 21, 1968), p. 1.

[18] Ellis, Minnesota address.

[19] Ellis, *The Beacon* (May 5, 1968), p. 6.

[20] E.g., Liturgy Committee, Nicodemus Club, Vincent de Paul Society, Cursillo, Lectors and Ushers, Altar and Rosary Society, Girl Scouts, Boy Scouts, Parent-Teacher Association, Altar Boys, teachers, tutors, and sports leaders.

[21] Ellis wrote at the close of 1965: "No matter what news captured the headlines, this will always be the year that I became Pastor of St. Cecilia's, the year that I married a people—for a Pastor is truly wedded to his people as Christ is to the Church" (*The St. Cecilia Weekly*, December 26, 1965).

[22] Sister M. Camille, RSM, "Life, Death and the Theology of Garbage," *The Beacon* (July 4, 1971), pp. 8–9.

[23] Father John Markham, funeral homily, St. Cecilia Parish, Detroit, Michigan, June 8, 1971.

[24] Joseph Fox, p. 70.

Chapter Six

[1] John Hart, *The Spirit of the Earth: A Theology of the Land* (New York, 1984), pp. 159–160.

[2] Wood, p. 102.

[3] Boff, p. 222.

[4] Joseph A. Fitzmyer, "The Letter to the Romans," in *The Jerome Biblical Commentary Vol. II,* ed. Raymond Brown, et al. (Englewood Cliffs, NJ, 1968), p. 316.

[5] Boff, p. 223.

[6] Berry, p. 36.

[7] Buber, pp. 58–59.

[8] R.M. Benedict Duss, OSB and R.M. Mary Aline Trilles de Warren, OSB, nuns of the Abbey of Jouarre, arrived from France on August 31, 1946 to found Regina Laudis. They were met by Benedictine Oblate and artist, Lauren Ford, who welcomed them into her home at Sheepfold, Connecticut. Coming from war-devastated France, the nuns arrived at Sheepfold with three cents and the vocation to found. Today the abbey, centered in a small, renovated brass factory building, extends through other abbey buildings, guest houses, fields and groves consonant with the intensity of Benedictine life.

[9] Abbey Christmas Essay, 1974.

[10] San Vincenzo is the second foundation begun by the nuns of Regina Laudis. Our Lady of the Rock Monastery, Shaw Island, Washington, was founded in 1976.

[11] Abbey Christmas Essay, 1989.

[12] Abbey Christmas Essay, 1989.

[13] See Leonard Weber, "Land Use Ethics: The Social Responsibility of Ownership," in *Theology of the Land,* ed. Bernard F. Evans and Gregory D. Cusack (Collegeville, MN, 1987), p. 19.

[14] Walter Bruggemann, "Land: Fertility and Justice," in *Theology of the Land,* p. 43.

[15] Dr. D. W. Caldwell, Seminar, Regina Laudis, June 5, 1969. Caldwell's observations and reverent interaction with rocks were echoed in a letter received by a graduate student in the abbey community who is working with heritage and with the "earth remembering." The Assistant Dean of The Union Institute responded to her "Learning Agreement" and shared his own experience:

> At one time I lived in the Willamette Valley in Oregon. I had to break up a virgin piece of ground for a large garden. As an agricultural field worker it was not unusual for me to do this kind of work yet at that moment the slicing of the spade through that thick, vigorous sod jarred me as if I shared the pain of the earth. This so moved me that I

lay spread-eagled on the thick sod to relieve the sense of pain. At that time as I realized I was asking the earth for forgiveness, I simultaneously "felt" the "earth thinking." From that experience I have since carried with me the presence of a "sentient earth." I mention my experience briefly in response to your quite elegant and far-reaching concept of the land remembering.

[16] Belden C. Lane, *Landscapes of the Sacred: Geography and Narrative in American Spirituality* (Mahwah, NJ, 1988), p. 17.

[17] Lane, p. 19.

[18] Hart, p. 55.

[19] Lane, p. 25.

[20] Abbey Christmas Essay, 1984.

[21] The animals are treated with individual respect. Each calf is named, often in relation to the feast or mystery celebrated in the liturgical year on the day of its birth. Children from the catechetical program, who witnessed the birth of "Palma" on Palm Sunday, were invited to return on Holy Thursday to see that the calf had survived and had bonded with its mother.

[22] A wry comment in the 1984 Abbey Christmas Essay synchronizes with the earlier discussion of incongruity within mutuality:

> Those who relate to Benedictines are driven mad by an aspect of our charism: when we speak to the advantage of another, we accent the limitation rather than the potential. No amount of rational explanation can turn this seeming negative into a positive. In their eyes it is an undercut. This fact puts us squarely in the position of not only living in the acknowledgment of opposites but of pressing through to their reconciliation in a new creation beyond either complement.

[23] Treatise on faith addressed to Peter by Saint Fulgentius of Aruspe. See *The Liturgy of the Hours,* Vol. II, pp. 383–384. The Indian Chief, Seattle, asks: "What is man without the beasts? If all the beasts were gone, man would die of great loneliness of the spirit–for whatever happens to the beasts also happens to man. All things are connected. Whatever befalls the earth befalls the sons of earth."

[24] Lane, p. 19.

Chapter Seven

[1] O'Donnell, *Mystery of the Triune God*, p. 166.

[2] Hans Urs von Balthasar, "Jesus, the Proof of the Triune Love of God for the World," in *The von Balthasar Reader*, ed. Medard Kehl and Werner Löser, trans. Robert J. Daly and Fred Lawrence (New York, 1982), p. 187.

[3] Teresa of Avila, *The Interior Castle*, VI: 7, 5, in *The Collected Works of St. Teresa of Avila Vol. II*, trans. Otilio Rodriguez and Kieran Kavanaugh (Washington, DC, 1980), p. 399.

[4] Teresa, VII: 1, 6, p. 430.

[5] Teresa, VII: 1, 7-8, pp. 430-431.

[6] Hart, pp. 157-158.

[7] Robert Brungs, "A Catholic Perspective 'On the Creation,'" paper given at The Institute for Theological Encounter with Science and Technology Seminar, 15-17 March, 1991, St. Louis, MO (p. 15).

Works Cited

Abbott, Walter M., ed. *The Documents of Vatican II.* Joseph Gallagher, trans. ed. New York: America Press, 1966.

Ashley, Benedict M. *Theologies of the Body: Humanist and Christian.* Braintree, MA: The Pope John Center, 1985.

Augustine, St. *The Trinity*. Stephen McKenna, trans. Washington, DC: The Catholic University of America Press, 1963.

Backman, E. Louis. *Religious Dances in the Christian Church and in Popular Medicine.* E. Classen, trans. Westport, CT: Greenwood Press, reprinted 1977.

Balthasar, Hans Urs von. "Christian Prayer." *Communio*, V, 1 (Spring 1978): 15–21.

"Being with the Poor." *In Letters from S. Egidio*, Community Newsletter (February 1989).

Bermejo, A. M. "Circumincession." *New Catholic Encyclopedia,* Vol. III, p. 880. San Francisco: McGraw-Hill Book Co., 1967.

Berry, Donald L. *Mutuality: The Vision of Martin Buber.* Albany, NY: State University of New York Press, 1985.

Boff, Leonardo. *Trinity and Society*. Maryknoll, NY: Orbis Books, 1988.

Bracken, Joseph A. *The Triune Symbol: Persons, Process and Community.* New York: University Press of America, 1985.

Brague, Rémi. "On the Christian Model of Unity: The Trinity." *Communio,* X, 2 (Summer 1983): 149–166.

Brinkman, B. R. "On Sacramental Man." *The Heythrop Journal,* five-part series, 1972–73.

——. "On Sacramental Man: II." *The Heythrop Journal,* XIV, 1 (January 1973): 5–34.

Brown, Raymond E. *The Gospel According to John I–XII.* Anchor Bible, Vol. 29. Garden City, NY: Doubleday and Co., 1966.

——. *The Gospel According to John XIII–XXI.* Anchor Bible, vol. 29A. Garden City, NY: Doubleday and Co., 1970.

Brungs, Robert A. *You See Lights Breaking Upon Us: Doctrinal Perspectives on Biological Advance.* St. Louis, MO: ITEST, 1989.

——. "A Catholic Perspective 'On the Creation.'" Paper given at The Institute for Theological Encounter with Science and Technology Seminar, St. Louis, MO, 15–17 March 1991.

Buber, Martin. *I and Thou.* Walter Kaufmann, trans. New York: Charles Scribner's Sons, 1970.

Camille, Sister M., RSM. "Life, Death and the Theology of Garbage." *The Beacon* (July 4, 1971): 8–9.

Cousins, Ewert. "A Theology of Interpersonal Relations." *Thought,* XLV, 176 (Spring 1970): 56–82.

Eichner, Sister Maura, SSND. *What We Women Know.* West Lafayette, IN: Sparrow Press, 1980.

Ellis, Father Raymond, Pastor, St. Cecilia Parish, Detroit, MI. Address to priests and religious educators of the Winona, Minnesota Diocese, February 22, 1971.

——. *The Beacon* (1968–69).

——. *The St. Cecilia Weekly* (1965).

Evans, Bernard F., and Gregory D. Cusack , eds. *Theology of the Land.* Collegeville, MN: The Liturgical Press, 1987.

Fitzmyer, Joseph A. "The Letter to the Romans." In *The Jerome Biblical Commentary Vol. II.* Raymond Brown et al., eds., 291–331. Englewood Cliffs, NJ: Prentice-Hall, Inc., 1968.

Forte, Bruno. *l'Eglise icône de la Trinité.* Paris: Médiaspaul, 1985.

Fortman, Edmund. *The Triune God: A Historical Study of the Doctrine of the Trinity.* Corpus Instrumentorum, Inc., 1972. Grand Rapids, MI: Baker Book House, 1982.

Fox, Joseph. "Toward a Theology of the Parish." Dissertation, Dominican House of Studies, Washington, D.C., n.d.

Freedman, David H. "Weird Science." *Discover,* XI, 11 (November 1990): 62–68.

Fry, Christopher. "The Lady's Not for Burning." In *Christopher Fry Plays,* 111–212. London: Oxford University Press, 1973.

Gallagher, Charles A., George A. Maloney, Mary F. Rousseau

and Paul F. Wilczak. *Embodied in Love: Sacramental Spirituality and Sexual Intimacy.* New York: Crossroad Publishing Co., 1983.

Gelpi, Donald L. *The Divine Mother: A Trinitarian Theology of the Holy Spirit.* Washington, DC: University Press of America, 1984.

Gibson, Rev. Arthur. "Heidegger, Camus, and the film Jules et Jim." Lecture at University of St. Michael's College, University of Toronto, winter term, 1974.

Gleick, James. *Chaos: Making a New Science.* New York: Penguin Books, 1987.

Gruenler, Royce Gordon. *The Trinity in the Gospel of John: A Thematic Commentary on the Fourth Gospel.* Grand Rapids, MI: Baker Book House, 1986.

Hart, John. *The Spirit of the Earth: A Theology of the Land.* New York: Paulist Press, 1984.

"Heard at the Conference." *Catholic International,* 2, 2 (16–31 January 1991): 93.

Hebblethwaite, Brian. "Perichoresis–Reflections on the Doctrine of the Trinity." *Theology,* LXXX, No. 676 (July 1977): 255–261.

Henrici, Peter. "Modernity and Christianity." *Communio,* XVII, 2 (Summer 1990): 141–151.

Hill, William. *The Three-Personed God: The Trinity as a Mystery of Salvation.* Washington, DC: The Catholic University of America Press, 1982.

"Holy Spirit." In *Harper's Bible Dictionary,* pp. 401–402. Paul J. Achtemeier, ed. San Francisco: Harper and Row, 1985.

Hug, James E., ed. *Tracing the Spirit: Communities, Social Action, and Theological Reflection.* New York: Paulist Press, 1983.

Irwin, James B., with William A. Emerson, Jr. *To Rule the Night.* Nashville, TN: Broadman Press, 1982.

Jerusalem Bible, The. Alexander Jones et al., eds. Garden City, NY: Doubleday and Co., 1966.

Jones, James W. "The Lure of Fellowship." *Cross Currents,* XXV, No.1 (Winter 1977): 420–423.

Kehl, Medard, and Werner Löser, eds. *The von Balthasar Reader.* Robert J. Daly and Fred Lawrence trans. New York: Crossroad, 1982.

Kelly, Anthony J. "Trinity and Process: Relevance of the Basic Christian Confession of God." *Theological Studies,* 31, 3 (1970): 393–414.

Kimmerling, Bernadette. "Marriage, Friendship and Community." *The Furrow,* 31, 6 (June 1980): 366–373.

Lane, Belden C. *Landscapes of the Sacred: Geography and Narrative in American Spirituality*. Mahwah, NJ: Paulist Press, 1988.

Lerner, Harriet Goldhor. *The Dance of Intimacy*. New York: Harper and Row, 1989.

Liturgy of the Hours, The, Vol. II. New York: Catholic Book Publishing Co., 1976.

Maloney, George A. "A Trinitarian Church of One in Many: A Mysticism of Community." *Diakonia,* XV, 1 (1980): 200–219.

Mertl, Steve. "Personal computer conduit for ultimate in safe sex." *The Star Phoenix,* June 13, 1992, p. E8.

O'Donnell, John J. *The Mystery of the Triune God.* New York: Paulist Press, 1989.

Ong, Walter. *Fighting for Life.* London: Cornell University Press, 1981.

Otilio Rodriguez and Kieran Kavanaugh, trans. eds. *The Collected Works of St. Teresa of Avila.* Washington, DC: ICS Publications, 1980.

Painton, Priscilla, and Elizabeth Taylor. "Love and Let Die." *Time,* 136, 12 (March 19, 1990): 52–58.

Pope John Paul II. "Apostolic Letter on Augustine of Hippo." Vatican trans. *Origins,* 16, 16 (October 2, 1986): 281–293.

——. *Blessed are the Pure of Heart.* Vatican trans. Boston, MA: Daughters of St. Paul, 1983.

——. "Holy Thursday Letter to Priests." Vatican trans. *Origins,* 18, 43 (April 6, 1989): 730–734.

——. *On the Holy Spirit in the Life of the Church and the World.* Issued 1986. Vatican trans. Boston, MA: Daughters of St. Paul, n.d.

——. *On the Mercy of God.* Issued 1980. Vatican trans. Boston, MA: Daughters of St. Paul, n.d.

——. *Original Unity of Man and Woman.* Vatican trans. Boston, MA: Daughters of St. Paul, 1981.

——. *Reflections on Humanae Vitae.* Vatican trans. Boston, MA: Daughters of St. Paul, 1984.

——. *The Redeemer of Man.* Issued 1979. Vatican trans. Boston, MA: Daughters of St. Paul, n.d.

——. *The Theology of Marriage and Celibacy.* Vatican trans. Boston, MA: Daughters of St. Paul, 1986.

———. *Vocation and Mission of the Lay Faithful.* Vatican trans. Sherbrooke, PQ: Les Editions Paulines, 1989.

———. *On the Renewal of the Religious Life According to the Teaching of the Second Vatican Council.* Vatican trans. Boston, MA: Daughters of St. Paul, 1971.

Pope Paul VI. *On the Renewal of the Religious Life According to the Teaching of the Second Vatican Council.* Boston, MA: St. Paul Editions, 1971.

Rahner, Karl, and Herbert Vorgrimler. *Theological Dictionary.* Cornelius Ernst. ed.; Richard Strachan, trans. New York: Herder and Herder, 1965.

Rahner, Karl, ed. *The Teaching of the Catholic Church.* Staten Island, NY: Alba House, 1967.

———. *Theological Investigations IV.* Kevin Smyth, trans. Baltimore, MD: Helicon Press, 1966.

Richard of St. Victor. "Book Three of the Trinity." In *Richard of St. Victor,* Grover A. Zinn, trans., 371–397. The Classics of Western Spirituality Series. Toronto: Paulist Press, 1979.

Sartre, Jean-Paul. *Being and Nothingness: An Essay on Phenomenological Ontology.* Hazel E. Barnes, trans. New York: Philosophical Library, Inc., 1956.

Schillebeeckx, Edward. *Christ the Sacrament of the Encounter with God.* New York: Sheed and Ward, 1963.

Schmitz, Kenneth. "Postmodern or modern-plus?" *Communio,* XVII, 2 (Summer 1990): 152–166.

Schneider, Richard. "The Human Person as the Image of the Three-Personal God." Lecture, Marquette University, Milwaukee, Wisconsin, August 8, 1966.

Sears, Robert T. "Trinitarian Love as Ground of the Church." *Theological Studies,* 37 (December 1976): 652–679.

Shook, L. K., ed. *Theology of Renewal Vol . I.* New York: Herder and Herder, 1968.

Soelle, Dorothee. "'Thou Shalt Have No Other Jeans Before Me' (Levi's Advertisement, Early Seventies): The Need for Liberation in a Consumerist Society." In *The Challenge of Liberation Theology: A First World Response,* Brian Mahan and L. Dale Richesin, eds., 4–16. Maryknoll, NY: Orbis Books, 1981.

Spiceland, James D. "Process Theology." In *One God in Trinity,*

Peter Toon and James D. Spiceland, eds., 133–157. Westchester, IL: Cornerstone Books, 1980.

"St. Egidio: What is it?" Information bulletin, n.d.

Steere, Douglas V. *Mutual Irradiation: A Quaker View of Ecumenism.* Pendle Hill Pamphlet 175, n.d.

"The Community of St. Egidio." Rome: Piazza S. Egidio, 3/a–00153 Roma, Italia, n.d.

Trible, Phyllis. *God and the Rhetoric of Sexuality.* Philadelphia: Fortress Press, 1978.

"Trinity of the Old Testament." *The Feasts of Rus: Icon Calendar Book.* Toronto: St. Paul Book and Media Centre, 1991.

Vogel, Arthur A. *Body Theology: God's Presence in Man's World.* New York: Harper and Row, 1973.

Wasserman, Aaron O. *Biology.* New York: Appleton-Century-Crofts, 1973.

Webster's Third New International Dictionary. Philip Babcock Gove and staff, eds. Springfield, MA: G. & C. Merriam Company, 1981.

Welch, Sharon D. *Communities of Resistance and Solidarity: A Feminist Theology of Liberation.* Maryknoll, NY: Orbis Books, 1985.

Wood, Nathan R. *The Trinity in the Universe.* Grand Rapids, MI: Kregel Publications, 1978.

Wright, Wendy M. *Bond of Perfection: Jeanne de Chantal & François de Sales.* New York: Paulist Press, 1985.

Wright, Wendy M. "Reflections on Spiritual Friendship Between Men and Women." Weavings, Nashville, TN, n.d.

Zaner, Richard M. *The Context of Self: A Phenomenological* Inquiry Using Medicine as a Clue. Athens, OH: Ohio University Press, 1981.

Index